THE MISSION FACTOR

Other books by Leland Wilson:

Living With Wonder

The Will Rogers Touch

Silver City

THE MISSION FACTOR

A STUDY GUIDE
to the
Church of the Brethren
Goals for the 80s

by Leland Wilson

Brethren Press: Elgin, Illinois

Illustrations from the chapel windows of Bethany
Theological Seminary, Oak Brook, Ill.
Photography by F. Wayne Lawson.

Cover design by Ken Stanley

Library of Congress Cataloging in Publication Data

Wilson, Leland.
   The mission factor.

   Includes bibliographies.
   1. Church of the Brethren—Doctrinal and controversial works—
Brethren authors.   I. Title.

BX7821.2.W54   230´.65   80-19102
ISBN 0-87178-575-7

To the irrepressible Michael

CONTENTS

GOALS FOR THE 80S
CHURCH OF THE BRETHREN

GOD, THE LORD OF ALL LIFE AND OF ALL CREATION CALL US

TO DO JUSTICE

- by witnessing to God's justice which forgives us and requires us to turn the other cheek and walk the second mile
- by altering our lifestyles to consume less and to share more, accepting the challenge of the simplicity of Jesus' life and mission
- by supporting efforts to establish a just world order through nonviolent means

—seeking the guidance of the Holy Spirit and studying prayerfully Isaiah 59; Amos 5; Matthew 5-7, 25; Luke 4; Revelation 4.

TO LOVE TENDERLY

- by sharing the good news of Jesus through proclamation and example
- by living at one with God, at peace with one's self, one's family, one's neighbor, and one's environment

- *by building community and wholeness in all aspects of life*
- *by confronting and caring for one another*
- *by claiming God's gift of reconciliation in the family, the church, society, and among all nations and all faiths*

—seeking the guidance of the Holy Spirit and studying prayerfully Genesis 1; Hosea 3, 11; Matthew 18, 28; Luke 10; Romans 12; 1 Corinthians 12, 13; 2 Corinthians 5; Galatians 6; Ephesians 4.

TO WALK HUMBLY

- *by diligently searching the scriptures*
- *by living as a servant people who know the empowering love exemplified by the basin and the towel*
- *by being in mission that lives out mutuality*
- *by celebrating the lordship of Christ and the interdependence of all humanity*

—seeking the guidance of the Holy Spirit and studying prayerfully Isaiah 53; Luke 7; John 13, 15, 17; Philippians 2.

INTRODUCTION

The 1979 Church of the Brethren Annual Conference adopted the goals statement that appears on the preceding page. Its headings are taken from the Micah passage and its twelve items identify areas to which the church feels called. The statement is obviously intended to be evocative, for at the end of each of the three sections, there is the admonition to actively seek "the guidance of the Holy Spirit" and to study prayerfully several listed chapters from the scripture. The Church affirmed in its resolution that "God, the Lord of all life and of all creation, calls us . . . "

The material which follows is intended to assist the Church of the Brethren in exploring the implications of the goals in focusing and centering upon the goals sufficiently that they become widely shared goals throughout the Church, and in providing encouragement toward achieving the goals. The book can be used personally, or it can form a guide for group study. The thirteen chapters can provide for a quarter of lessons in a church school class.

The chapters, except for the final chapter, each relate to an item in the goals statement. (Chapter 13 concerns the Micah passage.) Each chapter explores some aspect of the stated goal. In studying the goals, I very soon became aware that the goals were of such a general nature that I could not hope to be comprehensive. This means that *The Mission Factor* will need to be seen as one resource among many if we are to deal adequately with the goals statement.

The chapters have the following organization:

- A brief quote that is a pointed statement on the theme.
- A scripture reading or two, usually drawn from the chapters listed in the goals statement. (I have also felt free to use other scripture to give a context for the goal.) You will note that the scriptures listed with the goals are only at the end of each section and are not related to a specific goal; also, all of the references are to entire chapters. Such a manner of listing suggests to me that those who prepared the goals wanted to be certain that the scripture would not be stripped from its context. Having the entire chapters also adds to the fulness that scripture can contribute to our understanding of the goals.
- A quotation from a recent source that relates to the theme. These include statements, reports, and excerpts from books.
- A general commentary. This is the main body of the chapter and should provide background for studying both the scripture and the goal.
- Comments on the scripture texts.
- Comments on the quoted material.
- Suggested questions or ideas for thought and discussion.
- Suggested activities toward achieving the goal.
- Resources for further study.

This book has emerged from a faith community. The La Verne Church of the Brethren, which I serve as minister, is in the process of incorporating the goals into its own life. That has helped me to approach this project, not in a vacuum, but in the arena.

Several people have assisted me in identifying what should be covered, in selecting specific scripture passages, in suggesting related quotations, activities and resources. While I take responsibility for what is written, I want to acknowledge the help of Donna Arnold, S. Loren Bowman, Zeta R. Brandt, Chris Bucher, Ted Bushong, Vernard Eller, Steve Engle, Steve Gregory, Tom Harvey, Leona Ikenberry, Mary Kay Kremer, Paul E. Miller, Robert T. Neher, Melody Stallings, Robert Walker, William Willoughby and Patricia Wilson.

Also, I would acknowledge Bob Bowman, who has served as editor and offered helpful suggestions.

The "Goals for the 80s" are goals to which we have been called by our Church. In the years immediately ahead, they are to become our mission factor. God calls us. Let us respond.

LELAND WILSON
La Verne, California
March, 1980

To do justice

> *by witnessing to God's justice*
> *which forgives us and requires*
> *us to turn the other cheek and*
> *walk the second mile.*

1   A ROLLING JUSTICE

There can be no love without justice.

JOHN PAUL II

But let justice roll down like waters, and righteousness like an everflowing stream.

Amos 5:24

You have heard that it was said, "An eye for an eye and a tooth for a tooth." But I say to you, Do not resist one who is evil. But if any one strikes you on the right cheek, turn to him the other also; and if any one would sue you and take your coat, let him have your cloak as well; and if any one forces you to go one mile, go with him two miles. Give to him who begs from you, and do not refuse him who would borrow from you.

Matthew 5:38-42

While we were yet helpless, at the right time Christ died for the ungodly. Why, one will hardly die for a righteous man — though perhaps for a good man one will dare even to die. But God shows his love for us in that while we were yet sinners Christ died for us. Since, therefore, we are now justified by his blood, much more shall we be saved by him from the wrath of God. For if while we were enemies we were reconciled to God by the death of his Son, much more, now that we are reconciled, shall we be saved by his life. Not only so, but we also rejoice in God through our Lord Jesus Christ, through whom we have now received our reconciliation.

Romans 5:6-11

The Bible regards human life as a history in which God seeks to create a community of those who love him and one another, and who celebrate his love in a life of faithfulness and joy. The covenant with Israel is established as an act of God's love. Its structure is the human order which exhibits God's righteous purpose. God's righteousness is his justice, and his justice is manifest in his working to put down the unrighteous, expose idols, show mercy, and achieve reconciliation in a new order which expresses man's dignity as bearer of the divine image.

. . . the Bible sees the issues of human justice arising in the history of the Christian community as the people of God seek to bring peace and reconciliation to all men, and to show a special concern for the hurt, the needy, and the weak. Before God every Christian knows that he is the hurt, the needy, the weak person for whom there could be only condemnation, if there were no mercy in God's righteousness.

Daniel Day Williams
The Spirit and the Forms of Love

ELIE WIESEL is the contemporary writer and playwright whose work has most probingly searched the meaning of the holocaust. In his portrayal and exploration of life in its spiritual nature, I think this Jewish dramatist has no equal in the theatre in these years. Born in Germany, he was yet a child when he was torn from his home and taken to Birkenau, Auschwitz, Buna and Buchenwald concentration camps. He survived World War II, and became a journalist and writer in France. Later, he came to this country and became an American citizen. He and his wife and son live in New York City. He teaches at Boston University and is a writer of both fiction and non-fiction.

One of Wiesel's plays is called *The Trial of God,* and it concerns the justice of God. The setting is in 1649 in the Jewish community of Shamgorod. The Jews of Shamgorod have just suffered a pogrom. The only Jews left are an embittered old innkeeper and his daughter, who was raped and tortured. To that community come three players, and in the spirit of celebrating Purim, the three propose to hold a trial of God for permitting such evil to happen. The innkeeper, angry and loud, outraged at what he sees to be God's hostility, cruelty and indifference, is eager to be the prosecutor. But who will be the defense attorney?

> Avremel: *Misery of miseries . . . In the whole world, from east to west, from south to north, is there no one to plead on behalf of the Almighty? No one to speak for Him?*
> Yankel: *No one to justify His ways?*
> Avremel: *No one to sing His glory?*
> Mendel: *Poor King, poor mankind—one is as much to be pitied as the other . . . In the entire creation, from kingdom to kingdom and nation to nation, is there not one person to be found, one person to take the side of the Creator? Not one believer to explain His mysteries? Not one teacher to love Him in spite of everything, and love Him enough to defend Him against His accusers? Is there no one in the whole universe who would take the case of the Almighty God?*

Finally, a Stranger appears who defends the ways of God, a Stranger who is revealed at the drama's end to be Satan.

The Trial of God challenges me because the Stranger defends the justice of God in ways that I would defend. I find myself agreeing with the Stranger and congratulating him on the brilliance of his defense. Then, I am shattered when the Stranger is unmasked as Satan.

A few months after reading *The Trial of God,* I came upon a review of the play in *The Christian Century* (January 30, 1980), written by Robert McAfee Brown. The reviewer tells of hearing the drama from its author before publication, of the long time it has taken Brown to cope with the implications of the play and its final revelation. Already moved by the play, I found Brown's review helpful in suggesting some of the meaning. He found it an affirmative writing, first with a powerful negation and then with the positive. The negation is this: *"the arguments that justify God in the face of evil are not merely inadequate; they are diabolical."* When we use such arguments as justify the ways of God to humans, according to Brown, "we are doing the devil's work." The affirmative conclusion is from the character of the innkeeper who maintains his complaint against God, but, nevertheless, is willing to die rather than renounce God.

Surely the justice of God is not a simple idea for us to comprehend. Justice is often symbolized as a blindfolded woman with a set of balancing scales. But how totally inadequate is that portrayal of God's justice—and how limited it is in conceiving human justice.

We will look to the scripture passages and the quotation from Daniel Day Williams above to seek understanding of God's justice.

The Annual Conference statement calls us to do justice "by witnessing to God's justice which forgives us and requires us to turn the other cheek and walk the second mile." Implied in the statement is the idea that receiving God's justice requires something of us—we are to do justice. There are echoes here of Bonhoeffer's charge that the church sometimes offers "cheap grace". "Cheap grace" is defined in his book *The Cost of Discipleship* as

> the preaching of forgiveness without requiring repentance, baptism without church discipline, Communion without confession, absolution without personal confession. Cheap grace is grace without discipleship, grace without the cross, grace without Jesus Christ, living and incarnate."

Having experienced God's justice, we are to do justice. Doing justice is often associated with retribution or, at least, trying to "make the punishment fit the crime." Turning the other cheek and walking the second mile speak of neither retribution nor of punishment, but neither are they a soft and easy acceptance of injustice and evil; they are not a condoning of child abuse or character assassination.

In fact, turning the other cheek is a powerful and dynamic counterforce to injustice.

A court of law might have trouble dealing with the idea of forgiveness. There would be demands for something other than forgiveness. But God's justice and the justice to which we are called concerns forgiveness. This is quite a different matter from easy acceptance. It is different from overlooking the problem, the sin, or the crime. It does not mean forgetting. Rather, it is a costly remembrance of what has happened and a readiness to accept the consequence of what follows. The one who forgives feels the pain of the wrong, and accepts the pain, believing that the offender can come to a new, redeeming position. Turning the other cheek and walking the second mile are, therefore, not idle or passive activities. They symbolize an attitude, a posture, while something dynamic is taking place. They are transitional positions that open the way to reconciliation.

We are the beneficiaries of God's justice. How thankful we can be for that. It is beyond human justice and though many people envision God's justice as more unyielding and punitive than human justice, that is surely not the God revealed to us in Jesus Christ. The God who expects us to walk the second mile and to turn the other cheek, does no less for us. How unChrist-like it is to assume that God retaliates for each of our transgressions. Certainly, sin and evil exact their cost, but we do not live in a mechanical world in which the Creator follows the old law of "An eye for an eye and a tooth for a tooth" (Matthew 5:38). The grace in God's justice is the good news, and it is to that grace that we are called to give witness.

CONCERNING THE AMOS TEXT

Amos thunders his pronouncement on justice in what is one of the best known of statements from the prophets. A shepherd of Tekoa, Amos attacks evil in both the neighbors and among his own people. He declares rejection of pious words spoken in worship when there is no worship. Harsh words are directed at the affluent women of Samaria, "you cows of Bashan" (Amos 4:1), whose lavish living made a continual demand upon their husbands and who thus share responsibility for the oppression of the poor. Charges are leveled that Israel is an apostate people who pursue prosperity rather than the righteousness of God (Amos 5:5-12). With such a people, God repudiates their worship (Amos 5:21-23). It is in this setting that Amos issues the call, "But let justice roll down like waters, and righteousness like an everflowing stream."

This is a *rolling*, unfailing justice, justice that continues, like an "everflowing stream." This justice is not like a small trickle of water, but is full and generous like water rolling down from a waterfall.

By studying the prophet Amos, we should be clear that justice can and does involve confrontation in the process of making right what is wrong. That confrontation is found in his denunciation of those who take advantage of the poor.

CONCERNING THE MATTHEW TEXT

In the Sermon on the Mount, Jesus speaks of the way to live in the Kingdom. He brings a new interpretation to what is expected of the one who lives as God intends. Beginning with the Beatitudes, which reverse the usual understanding of what and who is important, there is a series of teachings that are "ethics of the kingdom." Some may dismiss them as impossible ideals, but these teachings have been basic instruction for Brethren. They are possible in Christ, and to that manner of living we are called.

In Matthew 5:38-42, Jesus addresses the idea of retaliation. He was familiar with the Mosaic code which prescribed, "If any harm follows, then you shall give life for life, eye for eye, tooth for tooth, hand for hand, burn for burn, wound for wound, stripe for stripe" (Exodus 21:23-25). This code provided a limitation on retaliation by requiring everyone offended to limit punishment to an equal injury. But Jesus rejected the whole business of calculating the sin of the offender and then punishing in like manner.

The point which Jesus makes is that the crime of another person should not determine your action. If a person has done evil to you, that is not license or justification for you to do a similar evil. Do not permit the violence of another person to provoke you to violence. The "second mile" comes from the general practice of Roman soldiers requiring citizens of a conquered country to carry their baggage one mile. If you are forced to go a mile, says Jesus, go two miles, because you can choose the second mile.

The Matthew passage points to a justice that is not tit-for-tat retaliation, but choosing to act rightly out of one's own conviction of what is right.

CONCERNING THE ROMANS TEXT

From Romans, we learn about God's justice to us. That is, God loves us, not on the basis that we deserve God's love (we were yet sinners), but for the sake of reconciliation. It is most difficult to accept the possibility that God accepts us as we are, or that God does not punish in retribution for each sin. But, Paul says that is what happened and that is the reason we can rejoice "in God through our Lord Jesus Christ."

CONCERNING THE WILLIAMS QUOTATION

The material above from Daniel Day Williams speaks of both God's justice and human justice. The writer describes the way in which God's justice is shown—by putting down the unrighteous, by exposing idols, by showing mercy, and by achieving reconciliation in a new human order of dignity. The Christian does justice by bringing peace and reconciliation to all, and by having a special concern for the hurt, the needy, and the weak. Williams notes that, before God, all Christians recognize their own need—the quotation ends in the same spirit as the Romans passage.

FOR FURTHER CONSIDERATION

• Read Psalm 59 which speaks of national wickedness, of God's displeasure in the absence of justice, and of God's justice being dispensed "according to their deeds . . . wrath to his adversaries, requital to his enemies." How does this Psalm fit into our understanding of God's justice?

• The 1980's will, in all likelihood, be marked by terrorist activities in many parts of the world. How do Christians witness to terrorists of God's justice and what does God require of us in dealing with terrorists?

• When you receive God's justice, what do you experience when you fail to "turn the other cheek" or "walk the second mile"?

• How is God's justice related to human justice?

• Some studies have shown that a large proportion of inactive members in the Church become inactive because they feel some grievance, some injustice. Do you know of inactive members with whom you should "walk the second mile"?

• One of the most violent institutions of our society is the family. To believe in God's justice is to witness to that justice and practice justice in the family. What do you see as the problems of justice involving male-female, parent-child, and grandparent relationships?

• Does God's justice have implications for international justice? How do Christians witness to God's justice to the nations of the world?

SOME ACTIVITIES

Plan an evening to read, as a group, Elie Wiesel's play, *The Trial of God*. If there are persons who could form a drama troupe, produce the play for the congregation. Follow the reading or production of the play with a discussion of your feelings about God as you experienced the play.

Read Dostoevsky's novel, *The Brothers Karamazov*, and study the difference in the characters of Ivan and Alyosha in how they respond to the reality and presence of evil, particularly the oppression of children.

Share with at least one other person this week an experience of grace that has come to you.

RESOURCES FOR ADDITIONAL STUDY

Bowman, Rufus. *Seventy Times Seven*. Elgin: Brethren Press, 1945.

Humphreys, Fisher. *Thinking About God*. New Orleans: Insight Press, 1974.

Swomley, John. "Liberation and Violence: The Case of Bonhoeffer," in *Liberation Ethics*. Riverside, N. J.: Macmillan, 1972.

Ward, James M. *Amos and Isaiah: Prophets of the Word of God*. Nashville: Abingdon, 1969.

Wiesel, Elie. *The Trial of God*. New York: Random House, 1979.

Williams, Daniel Day. *The Spirit and the Forms of Love*. New York: Harper-Row, 1968.

To do justice
    by altering our lifestyles to
    consume less and to share
    more, accepting the challenge
    of the simplicity of Jesus' life
    and mission.

2 LIFESTYLE MODELS

The Brethren are a plain people.
They dress modestly and decently.
What more than this is held to
be a violation of the plain pre-
cepts of the New Testament.
MARTIN G. BRUMBAUGH

Therefore I tell you, do not be anxious about your life, what you shall eat or what you shall drink, nor about your body, what you shall put on. Is not life more than food, and the body more than clothing? Look at the birds of the air: they neither sow nor reap nor gather into barns, and yet your heavenly Father feeds them. Are you not of more value than they? And which of you by being anxious can add one cubit to his span of life? And why are you anxious about clothing? Consider the lilies of the field, how they grow; they neither toil nor spin; yet I tell you, even Solomon in all his glory was not arrayed like one of these. But if God so clothes the grass of the field, which today is alive and tomorrow is thrown into the oven, will he not much more clothe you, O men of little faith? Therefore do not be anxious, saying "What shall we eat?" or "What shall we drink?" or "What shall we wear?" For the Gentiles seek all these things; and your heavenly Father knows that you need them all. But seek first his kingdom and his righteousness, and all these things shall be yours as well.

Therefore do not be anxious about tomorrow, for tomorrow will be anxious for itself. Let the day's own trouble be sufficient for the day.

Matthew 6:25-34

Why are so many people not living the modest, simple life? Too often they are not willing to make the sacrifice. They have been permitted to have their own way so long, the simple life does not appeal to them. When they were children, they had what they wanted. The parents forgot that "as the twig is bent the tree's inclined." If you are one of these you deserve sympathy. Children can not hope to live selfish, worldly lives, and change easily when they grow up. The moral virtues must be practiced. In eating and drinking only the needs of the body should be satisfied. Too often we hold out for the desire of the carnal mind. So many people lay foundations of selfishness which they are never quite able to break. The simple life can not be lived if we have not a proper background. We need to cultivate a proper attitude toward others. Because we are not our own, we should put self in the background for the sake of others. A proper respect for our parents is needful, as well as a right disposition toward God, prayer and the time and place of worship. . . . To live the simple and natural life is not easy. Social life and customs are confusing. Modern business creates many perplexing situations. Even the home life often becomes a trial. New customs come into our community and various agencies of progress are constantly being introduced. These often revolutionize life. What must be the Christian's attitude toward these things? We must of necessity enter into some of these conditions. We may use the agencies of progress, but must not abuse them. Let them contribute to real moral and religious culture; then they will not lead us away from the truth.

D. W. Kurtz, S. S. Blough, C. C. Ellis
Studies in Doctrine and Devotion

WE ARE in a time of recovery of the simple life. While that thread has been woven consistently into our fabric, the recent decades have muted its color.

We can be quite clear that the simple life has been a part of our heritage. It was an integral part of the mind of those movements which gave birth to the Church of the Brethren. The Anabaptists "renounced earthly comfort and glory. Personal adornment, worldly amusements, wealth, and all forms of luxury were regarded as inconsistent with the Christian life. Standards of admission and discipline were severe" (Floyd Mallott, *Studies in Brethren History*). The Pietists emphasized the embodiment of love in everyday life. They advocated reading the Bible and simple preaching. There was a reaction to the scholasticism and formality of the institutional church. Following Jesus Christ, Pietists contended, was a matter of inner experience. It did not end there, but must become a matter of everyday living.

Edward K. Ziegler in *Simple Living* has a chapter which reviews the history of "A Plain People." He offers this perspective:

The combination of a rugged environment and a biblical concern for a simple following of Christ in all things created a frugal, relatively uncluttered and unsophisticated style of living. The simple life was for most Brethren an economic and social necessity, and they considered it a Christian virtue. As time went on, the attractions of affluence began to threaten the life-style which once had been a baptized necessity. Then, lest the advantages of maintaining unity in the church and a "gospel simplicity" be lost, the Brethren fell into a legalism which turned the outward forms of simple living into rigid membership requirements. Thus there came a flood of rules and legislative Annual Conference decisions which canonized the forms of simple living.

Especially, the simple life was symbolically centered around the matter of clothing and jewelry. Codes were developed and prescribed, so that dress styles became "separate from the world" and distinguished from the neighbors. The attire was functional, non-decorative; jewelry was prohibited. Even in the 1980's, many Brethren identify their simple life in the way they dress. Some wear the "plain clothes," and others wear simply plain clothing. And among all the Brethren, it is rare to see lavish or exotic or ornately jeweled dress.

The simple life referred not merely to dress, but also to the furnishing of our homes and our meeting houses, and to all of our possessions.

The simple life was advocated as essential in following the example and teachings of Jesus. It was a practical application of one's faith and a living testimony to one's beliefs. So strongly is the simple life imbedded into our character, that we are troubled by seeing those who identify themselves as Christian, and yet do not live simply. We respond most to those in whom we see simplicity—Ora Huston or Dan West or M. R. Zigler—and beyond to persons like Sister Theresa. Recent attempts in deliberate simple living or in building communities of simple living bear a strong witness to the whole church—even among those who would not choose such a lifestyle for themselves.

Some clarification should be made about this simple living. *It is not the same as living in poverty.* Sometimes there is a romanticizing of the poor—as if they are free from the worries of the rest of the world, as if they can more easily be faithful. It is true that Jesus had a bias on behalf of the poor, that he came to preach good news to the poor. The extent to which this is true can be seen in Robert McAfee Brown's theology as "The View From Below." Writing in the magazine *A.D.* in September 1977, Brown said he found himself re-reading the scripture and the world. In the 1940's he had to re-read through Jewish eyes. In the 1950's and the early 60's, he re-read through the eyes of blacks. In the mid- and late 60's, he used the eyes of the Vietnamese, and now he tries to see as Third World nations. When these people read scripture, they do so with "the view from below," and Brown thinks their reading in many cases is more accurate than his own, *"Because where they are coming from is where scripture has come from.* Scripture is written from their point of view. The Bible was written by oppressed people and for oppressed people with a promise from God that the oppression will be overcome." In this, Brown concludes, "The God of the Bible has a clear bias toward the poor." And he quotes that giant from earlier in this century, Karl Barth:

> God always takes his stand unconditionally and passionately on this side and this side alone: against the lofty and on behalf of the lowly; against those who already enjoy right and privilege and on behalf of those who are denied it and deprived of it.

That bias toward the poor is not that the poor should remain in poverty, but that they be delivered from poverty. *The simple life is not poverty.* In the early 70's, it became fashionable for the radical to assume the trappings of poverty. The children of the middle class wore frayed jeans and untrimmed hair as a protest against middle class values and as an identification with the poor. But that is quite a different matter from being poor. At any moment, they could choose to step out of poverty. The living conditions of the poor, who have no resources to consume, are poor of necessity and not by choice. The living conditions of the simple life, wherein there is an emphasis upon nonconsumption, are by choice. By living the simple life we are able to share more with the poor.

The simple life does not mean cheapness. If one examines the lifestyle of the early Brethren, I believe that it will be found that their possessions had quality. Their farms had good soil. Their crafts were performed with skill. Their homes and barns were well built, not shoddy and cheap. Many of their homes were built of large size to accommodate meetings of the church. And can you imagine a better, more generous meal than you would eat when hosted by one of the Pennsylvania Brethren? While the possessions were few, and while they were not intended as display or to be the treasure of this life, I believe that the simple living Brethren invested in quality, probably a more economical step in the end.

In the first breath, the simple life is not about things or possessions. *The simple life means singleness of purpose: the worship of God.*

Before we breathe the second breath, though, we must begin to relate the simple life to material things so that those things do not impede our single purpose. Questions about specific possessions or specific dress cannot be answered by a code or a table, but must probe what is the meaning involved and how are they used. And, possessions should be purchased and viewed with the church's call to us to consume less and to share more.

Many tell us that we will change lifestyles only when we are forced to do so. That is, we will lessen the pollution of the air by automobile emissions only when gasoline is no longer available, or when the cost becomes so great that we cannot afford to buy such great quantities of gasoline. And, from external pressures, we are now changing the size of cars we drive and the way we heat our homes. Some of the changes that we are making due to scarcity do not mean that life will be less. If we begin to walk where once we drove, who would say that life is poorer for that? If we begin to eat less, or to develop new diets, who would think our life is therefore impoverished? If we purchase fewer manufactured goods and develop more our own arts and crafts, is that a loss? If our housing patterns force us into higher density living, with less privacy, can there be positive elements in that? True, many of these changes we would make only when forced to do so; but forced adaptations are often God's way of revealing truth to us.

Some changes toward simplicity are being imposed upon us.

Beyond that, it is both possible and desirable to alter our lifestyles voluntarily as a positive choice because of our Christian calling.

Nine years ago, eight young couples in the La Verne congregation, after months of study, adopted and signed a "Corporate Statement on Christian Life-Style." They began:

> As twentieth-century Christians, we face the same basic dilemma which has confronted every preceding generation of Christians. We are caught between the demands of the Gospel and man's self-centered desires. But given the world situation as it is today, we must ask how we are to be faithful followers of Christ. We, as members of the La Verne Church of the Brethren, have been struggling with this question for several months. We have studied the Christian faith and the critical problems which we now face. It is our conviction that in view of our commitment to Christ, and awareness of the tremendous problems which must be solved, a change in our own life-style is imperative. Therefore, we have outlined some basic elements of the style of life which we believe to be demanded of us.

They indicated that they had no naive expectations that what they were doing would "bring in the kingdom," but they wished as individuals and as families to take seriously the changes demanded in their faith. They pledged themselves to support each other and, if necessary, to reprimand.

Their statement reviewed the crisis which we face of over-population and the destruction of our environment. They challenged the orthodoxy of "more means better," and criticized the measuring of a person's value by material affluence. There was a theological perspective, seeing God as Creator and human responsibility for shaping and using creation in a constructive way. They pointed to the biblical teachings of the corporateness of the human community and the responsibility for the neighbor. Regarding the "simple life" they said:

> An aspect of the Brethren heritage that needs to be resurrected and redefined is the concept of the "simple life." In its better moments, this theme has been a help in defining the kind of uncluttered life which is demanded by the Christian faith. In its more demonic moments, the "simple life" has been the basis for self-righteousness and exclusivity. It is our desire to interpret the "simple life" with the former intention.

With such orientation, they pledged themselves to father or mother no more than two children; if more children were desired, they would be adopted. Those who already had two children pledged to have no more. After two children, they said, "We will strongly encourage each other to seriously consider sterilization as a positive birth control measure which will prevent worry, accidents, and lapses of will."

The couples pledged to constantly re-evaluate their needs versus their wants in order to consume less. Wherever possible, they would use only products that could be recycled. They would buy lasting products rather than items that would need to be replaced frequently. Where feasible, they would share property such as lawnmowers and garden tools.

Along with this change in consumption, they recommitted themselves to be active members of the church.

Each of the sixteen people signed. And it soon became evident to the whole church that a new dynamic was at work in these people. They were alive to each other and to their neighbors. They took much more leadership in the church, and while financial pledging to the church was not a part of the statement, their pledges and giving increased dramatically.

Something of the nature of our world is indicated in the fact that only three of the eight couples are now a part of our congregation. The rest have moved to various parts of the country. Some time ago, they released each other from the specifics of their statement. But I sense that the same values and concerns continue to be important to them. And I know that for three or four years, their statement had a major impact upon their lives and also affected by its witness the rest of us in the congregation.

There are two New Testament models of lifestyles that we should study. Those two will not give us specific answers on how much and what to consume or on family size. But they do offer a perspective. The two models are John the Baptist and Jesus.

Jesus has always been considered a model. In fact, being a Christian has been thought to be a matter of being *in his steps*. And Jesus gives quite an endorsement of John: "Among those born of women there has arisen no one greater than John the Baptist" (Matthew 11:11). That should make John a worthy model.

We see the difference in lifestyles of the two men when they are compared with each other. John was a rough, earthy man. His dress and his manner were honest and abrasive. He kept the ceremonial laws. He confronted power in the way of the prophets. It is likely that John was a Nazirite, that is, he was set apart for God's service. Symbolic of that commitment, he was to drink no alcoholic drink and no razor was to come to his head—this as prescribed in Numbers 6. John seemed to live an austere existence and was confrontive.

Jesus was not a purist in keeping the ceremonial laws, and to some, he seemed lax. John came neither eating nor drinking, but "the Son of man came eating and drinking, and they say, 'Behold, a glutton and a drunkard, a friend of the tax collectors and sinners!' " (Matthew 11:19). Jesus identified himself among the poor, saying, "Foxes have holes, and birds of the air have nests; but the Son of man has nowhere to lay His head" (Luke 9:58). But he had friends who were wealthy and was supported by women of financial means (Luke 8:1-3). Jesus accepted the lavish gift of ointment poured on his head, so expensive that it was a scandal to his disciples. They called it a waste, but he called it beautiful (Matthew 26:6-13). He was concerned for the poor and the hungry, but he also enjoyed a feast. The clothing he wore was of fine quality (John 19:23). We have often called him a peasant, but as the son of a carpenter, he came from what would be comparable to a middle class home. While Jesus suffered, there is also a spontaneous, festive quality about him. Even his first miracle was performed at a wedding feast, turning water into wine. In *The Brothers Karamazov,* Dostoevsky says that Jesus performed his first miracle for the sake of gladness. Jesus could be confrontive and often was, but he also had a deeply compassionate side.

Jesus, himself, in telling the parable of child's play in Luke 7:31-35, contrasts the lifestyle of the two men. The people of this generation who reject God, he says, find a reason, a self-justification. They reject because of the lifestyle and the personality of the bearer of the message. They reject John because he was too ascetic; he came to them like a funeral. ("We wailed, and you did not weep.") They reject Jesus because he was not ascetic enough. He came to them life a wedding. ("We piped to you, and you did not dance.")

I believe that both Jesus and John offer lifestyle models. Both of them were of consuming zeal. Both had elements of strong independence. Both were prophets who began their ministry calling for repentance. John, especially, reflects austerity for the sake of the Gospel. Jesus, especially, reflects compassion for those in need. He was "good news to the poor" (Luke 4:18). Some of the most radical advocates of the simple life seem to be nearer to John than to Jesus in tone and emphasis and in the form of simplicity. I believe both models of lifestyle are faithful responses to God's calling. The question that remains is whether they will become models for us.

CONCERNING THE MATTHEW TEXT

The Matthew text comes from the "Sermon on the Mount" series of teachings. Jesus is instructing the disciples on living the religious life. "Do not be anxious," he tells them. "God gives life, will he not give food? God created your body—would not God see to clothing your body?" Thus, Jesus begins with an argument of more to less—that is, God has done the greater thing; will he not also do the lesser? Then he turns to nature and argues that the God who cares for the birds of the air and spreads the fields with lilies will care for you as a human, because you are worth more to God than these other elements in creation.

Jesus calls upon his followers to make priorities. "Seek first his kingdom and his righteousness . . . " That is the singleness of purpose; when that singleness is present, the other parts of life will follow.

"Take one day at a time," Jesus says. Do not become anxious about what might happen. Get through the day, and then face tomorrow the anxieties of that day.

This whole section calls upon us to trust God to provide our most basic needs. What a liberating message this can be to persons who become burdened by what might happen.

Apply this teaching to everyday life. Does it advocate that we "neither sow nor reap nor gather into barns"? Does it say, that we should not worry about what happens to future generations? Does it mean for the hungry of the world that if they are sufficiently devotional, they will be fed? If these are not meant, what is meant for the unemployed, the industrialist, the student?

CONCERNING THE SIMPLE LIFE TEACHING

Studies in Doctrine and Devotion was published in 1919. Then, sixty years ago, there was already the lament that many were not living the modest, simple life. The quoted passage attributes this lack to the indulgence of children.

Do you agree that the simple life cannot be lived if we do not have a proper background? Note that respect for parents and the devotional life are included as part of the living of the simple life.

The tension between emerging modern life and the simple life was recognized. The writers mention "various agencies of progress," but we would likely now be reluctant to attribute what is happening to "progress."

FOR FURTHER CONSIDERATION

• In what way was the life and mission of Jesus "simple"?

• To what extent should lifestyles be entirely an individual matter, and to what extent should the congregation become involved in shaping lifestyles?

• How can your conservation affect what is available to others?

• Identify several contemporary lifestyles as illustrated in well-known persons. Ask if those are simple lifestyles.

• How are holistic health and meditation related to a simple lifestyle?

• Should the limitation of family size be a part of our simple life teaching?

• Is the simple lifestyle an uniquely Christian emphasis?

SOME ACTIVITIES

Project yourself ahead to the year 2000 A.D. Describe your lifestyle and then narrate the history of how you arrived at that lifestyle.

Plan for ways to share appliances and tools among persons in the congregation. Create a resource inventory of things that members would be willing to loan.

Make a list of the lifestyle changes you have made in the past three years. Make a second list of lifestyle changes you want to make in the next three years.

Plan for a Sunday of worship in which every person (physically able) within a mile would walk to church, and every person beyond a mile would travel by public transportation or by car pooling with others in the congregation. In other words, try to avoid a single family driving to church alone.

Work with your Stewardship and Finance Commission to achieve the Annual Conference goal of doubling your giving by the end of the next decade so that by 1989, members will be giving at least 5% of their income through the Church; and work toward commitment to a higher level of Brotherhood Fund support.

RESOURCES FOR ADDITIONAL STUDY

Eller, Vernard. *The Simple Life*. Grand Rapids: Eerdmans, 1973.

Gish, Art. *Beyond the Rat Race*. New Canaan, Conn.: Keats, 1973.

Longacre, Doris. *More-With-Less-Cookbook*. Scottdale, Pa.; Herald Press, 1976.

Mallott, Floyd. *Studies in Brethren History*. Elgin: Brethren Press, 1954.

Meadows, Donella H. *Limits to Growth*. New York: Universe, 1974.

Petry, Ronald D. *Partners in Creation*. Elgin: Brethren Press, 1979.

Schumacher, E. F. *Small Is Beautiful*. New York: Harper-Row, 1976.

Yoder, Glee. *Passing on the Gift*. Elgin: Brethren Press, 1978.

Ziegler, E. K. *Simple Living*. Elgin: Brethren Press, 1974.

To do justice
    by supporting efforts to
    establish a just world order
    through nonviolent means.

3

A JUST ORDER

The Kingdom of God stands as the ultimate horizon of (the) future hope of man.
ROSEMARY RADFORD RUETHER

And Jesus, full of the Holy Spirit, returned from the Jordan, and was led by the Spirit for forty days in the wilderness, tempted by the devil. And he ate nothing in those days; and when they were ended, he was hungry. The devil said to him, "If you are the Son of God, command this stone to become bread." And Jesus answered him, "It is written, 'Man shall not live by bread alone.'" And the devil took him up, and showed him all the kingdoms of the world in a moment of time, and said to him, "To you I will give all this authority and their glory; for it has been delivered to me, and I give it to whom I will. If you, then, will worship me, it shall all be yours." And Jesus answered him, "It is written, 'You shall worship the Lord your God, and him only shall you serve.'" And he took him to Jerusalem, and set him on the pinnacle of the temple, and said to him, "If you are the Son of God, throw yourself down from here; for it is written, 'He will give his angels charge of you, to guard you,' and 'On their hands they will bear you up, lest you strike your foot against a stone.'" And Jesus answered him, "It is said, 'You shall not tempt the Lord your God.'" And when the devil had ended every temptation, he departed from him until an opportune time.

Luke 4:1-13

The world confronts us with the temptation to use violence in war, to acquiesce and participate in structural violence, and to support violent revolution against structural violence. Although we seek to identify with the oppressed, to these three types of violence we make a uniform response: the scriptures call us to reject all forms of violence and to undertake nonviolent acts to exercise our commitment to human liberation and justice. We must be vigilant against that which would seduce us to use the very means against which we must struggle. Such a nonviolent response is rooted in the call to radical discipleship; it calls us to take risks and to transform our own lives and human institutions for the sake of God's justice but it does not destroy life or close off the possibility of genuine reconciliation (nurtured in mishpat *and* shalom*) with an oppressor after the oppression is ended.*

We cannot retreat from the world. We are to move from where we are to where God's power and purpose have begun to define new possibilities and new necessities. We must become aware of the rampant injustice and subtle hidden violence in today's world, examine our own involvement, and identify nonviolently with the oppressed and suffering.

We must develop a theology of living here and now in the spirit of the kingdom. We look toward a future that will be more peaceful, just, and respectful of God's creation. We who are of the body of Christ, an incarnation of God's reconciling and redeeming love in the world, are called to be a channel of God's loving justice. Wherever brokenness among people exists, we are called to participate in God's work of healing; wherever people suffer from oppression, we are to work for God's act of liberation; and wherever people are deprived of basic human needs and opportunities, we are called to God's work of humanization. We are called to live the life of God's agape in the world because Christ is our Lord.

1977 Church of the Brethren Annual Conference
Statement on Justice and Nonviolence

A RECENT STUDY by Business International, a New York based firm, called attention to a rising tide of terrorism in the world. In the last decade, terrorists threatened the lives of many people and extorted some $125 million from American corporations and another $500 million from multi-national corporations. In the overwhelming majority of the worldwide attacks, the victims were Americans and the targets were businesses. In forecasting the world business climate, Business International warned that the level of terrorist activity will likely increase, as well as the level of violence and the sophistication of the terrorists.

Foreign policy is being conducted by savage attacks upon an embassy, usually not by a host government, but often with the acquiescence of the government in power. Hostages are held and threatened to secure certain actions from other governments.

The nations of the world are having an increasingly difficult time maintaining control within their own boundaries.

At this point, it appears likely that the 1980's will be a time of selected terrorism—that is, violence that will come in scattered places, without warning and without expectation. The spread of nuclear knowledge, through nuclear power and nuclear weapons, makes this terrorism even more ominous. And there is really no defense against acts of terrorism.

We may have in our national arsenal the equivalent of some 650,000 bombs the size of the one which leveled Hiroshima in 1945, but those bombs were powerless to release hostages in Iran. We may live in a world that spends $425 billion a year for the military, but that does not make us feel safe. In fact, as the level of armaments rises, the less safe we are, the less safe we feel. C. P. Snow has said that if the arms race continues as it is today, it is not a probability that the bombs will go off, it is a mathematical certainty.

We are threatened with violence by both terrorist groups and governments throughout the world. At the same time, most Americans benefit from a more subtle form of violence that keeps present power and wealth from being equitably distributed to the people of the world. This kind of violence is not directed toward territorial expansion; it is related, rather, to resource development and control. The most powerful and wealthy nations see access to these resources as "in our vital interests."

In the decade of the 1980's, one of the needs to which the Church must respond is the need for order. Not just any kind of order. An order is needed that will be supportive of human freedom and justice. Order is a political condition, and it is typically difficult and divisive when the Church confronts a political issue. There are those who believe that "the Church must stay out of politics." They are offended when the pulpit speaks concerning some current political issue and they feel that political positions are inappropriate for a Church Board or a Church of the Brethren General Board resolution. Usually, opposition to considering something political is accompanied with an appeal to "present Jesus Christ and him crucified," and him only.

The reason, I believe, that Christians have difficulty considering something political in a church context is that they have a greater loyalty to their political beliefs than to their religious beliefs; they identify more with a political party than with the Church. If we present Jesus Christ fully, he will be presented in a context that includes government. He will be related to the nations of the world. The Church must avoid becoming identified with candidates or parties, but must seek to be more partisan where matters of justice and peace are concerned.

The Christian is on the side of order. The metaphor which Jesus typically used to describe what it is like to live as God intends, was *kingdom.* That is a political term. It implies a realm in which there is order. The teaching of Jesus so far as order within the state is concerned, is indirect. He lived in an occupied country, but he did not accept the option of the Sadducees, that of collaboration. Nor did he accept the option of the Pharisees which would have been a theocracy. He appeared more at home with the Zealots, even numbering them among his disciples. Yet, Jesus strongly denounced any attempt to overthrow the state with violence. Nor did he take a position of anarchy. There appears to be an acceptance of the state in paying taxes, in making judgments, and in respecting laws.

Often cited in any discussion of church and state issues is that statement by Jesus, "Render therefore to Caesar the things that are Caesar's, and to God the things that are God's" (See Matthew 22:15-22; Mark 12:13-17; Luke 20:20-26). The statement needs to be seen as a response when there is an effort to entrap Jesus. Certainly it does not imply equal authority to Caesar and to God. But at least it does offer some recognition of the legitimacy of the state and its function. The 1967 Annual Conference of the Church of the Brethren says that the Caesar passage

> must never be taken to mean that God does not care what Caesar does or leaves undone. Government policy helps to determine whether there will be war or peace, justice or injustice, depression or inflation, affluence or poverty, and similar basic conditions of life. In such issues God cares, and the church, to the degree that it has the Spirit of God, also cares. Indeed, under God, both state and church are to be the instruments for expressing love of neighbor.

The writings of Paul are concerned with order. His pervasive and definitive statement on the state is found in Romans 13. A reading of this chapter makes clear that Paul recognizes the validity of government. He counsels a conscientious obedience to government and warns against anarchy. It is this passage, perhaps more than any other in the New Testament, that has made Christianity on the other side from disorder and anarchy. John Bennett has said, in *Christians and the State*, "The warning against anarchy because of the unruliness of men's sin is one of the prominent emphases in all Christian thinking about the state."

For Paul, the basic issue is found in the source of power of the ruling authorities. In obeying the state, it is not government, first of all, that the Christian obeys. The Christian obeys God, first of all, because the power and the authority of the state comes from God. The Christian bears all of the responsibilities of citizenship. Even though Christians live in a kingdom "not of this world," that spiritual citizenship does not terminate citizenship among neighbors. Our commitment to Christ does not relieve us of obligation to the state.

The Romans passage sounds quite absolute. It would seem that the Christian would be bound to obey the government no matter how unjust the command or the law. But that is a surface reading. It is precisely in Romans 13 that Karl Barth found the basis for civil disobedience. Barth understands earthly powers to be subject to the Divine Order. When civil authorities depart from the Divine Order, Christians honor them best by criticizing them, even disobeying them, if needed, to remain true to the Divine Order that the rulers have forsaken (See Karl Barth, *Community, State and Church*).

In 1967, the Church of the Brethren Annual Conference made a statement regarding "The Church's Attitude Toward the State." That statement is partially drawn from an understanding of Paul's Roman letter. Note the interest of the church in "maintaining order."

The Church affirms the institution of government as ordained of

God (Romans 13:1), necessary as an instrument for maintaining order, securing justice and freedom, and promoting the general welfare. The state and its citizens are under God and ultimately accountable to him as Creator, Sustainer, Sovereign Lord, and Judge. The sovereignty of the state is limited by the sovereignty of God. Moreover, the policy makers of the state share the sin and fallibility of mankind, and their decisions cannot be considered infallible. While the state may demand reasonable obedience, it may not demand absolute obedience, which belongs to God.

There are other New Testament passages that can be studied to understand the biblical perspective: I Corinthians 6; I Timothy 2:1, 2; and I Peter 2:13, 14. Finally, the Book of Revelation portrays the state as a beast. It reflects a power that has gone to excess by taking unto itself what belongs to God. It is interesting that the early Brethren in Europe, known as outlaws and outcasts wherever they went, still did not choose the image of the beast or the Book of Revelation as their primary understanding of the state.

Recent decades have found a large number of the Brethren resisting or not cooperating with the state as a way of being obedient to God's will for them. In the early 1960's, many Brethren became a part of the civil rights movement and disobeyed the racially discriminatory laws of a municipality or a state in response to a "higher law." During the Vietnam War, the Church said that one of the ways to fulfill the historic teaching of the Church against participating in war was noncooperation with the military draft. Currently, there are many who are led to a refusal to pay that portion of their taxes that supports war and many are actively supporting the establishment of a World Peace Tax Fund, to which payments for peaceful purposes might be made in place of taxes for war. Thus, within the need for order, the Church has recognized instances when the Christian is called to the "disorder" of disobedience as a way of being obedient to God. Civil disobedience, a 1969 Annual Conference statement said, "should be considered only after all legal means to correct injustice have failed." Further counsel has been that it be consistently nonviolent and that it be open, with civil authorities well aware of what is happening and with the individual ready to accept responsibility for the disobedient act. Obviously, there is a great amount of order in such disobedience.

The need for order within the nation is well recognized. The life-and-death problem that faces humanity is that there is *anarchy* in the world. We do not have a world order. Each nation presses its own sovereignty. There is no accountability to the entire human family. There is a World Court, but the court is largely powerless to implement its findings. There is a United Nations, performing many international services, a forum for world diplomacy, but quite clearly not a world government. Commercial interests maintain a form of order in the world, but those interests have revealed themselves to be exploitive and clearly represent the powerful at the expense of the weak.

The Christian must extend the concern for order to include the whole world. That order would provide the security that is essential for peoples everywhere to live full lives, unthreatened by the holocaust of all-out combat by nuclear powers.

Jacques Ellul, the French lay theologian, has explored the pervasive nature of violence, contending that "every state is founded on violence and cannot maintain itself save by and through violence" (Jacques Ellul, *Violence*). From this violence there are certain consequences. The first is continuity: a revolution born in violence maintains itself with violence for a generation or two. The second consequence is reciprocity ("All who take the sword shall perish by the sword" [Matthew 26:52]): violence prompts violence in opposition. The third consequence is sameness: that is, all violence is the same, the justified and the unjustified. The fourth consequence is that violence begets violence —*nothing else:* violence never creates liberty or justice. A fifth consequence of violence is that those who use violence always try to justify themselves and the use of violence.

Ellul contends that despite the fact that violence has been natural and a normal part of our human society, the Christian is called to nonviolence. The Christian "must struggle against violence precisely *because,* apart from Christ, violence is the form that human relations normally and necessarily take."

Ellul's understanding of violence clarifies the necessity for a nonviolent approach to world order, if that order is to be nonviolent and if it is to be just. The creation of such an order is the greatest political task to which we are called.

Concerning the Lukan Text

If you were to choose one chapter in the entire Bible which brings the most understanding to the life and ministry of Jesus Christ, I believe you could do no better than the fourth chapter of Luke.

First of all, people are very much revealed by their temptations, their testings. Where is the struggle in the person's life? If the temptation of the person is to steal or to rape, that tells much about the person. If the testing concerns competing approaches to how life is to be lived, how one's power and influence will be used, that is also very revealing. And this is the case with Jesus in the temptation scene; he is resolving the person he is to be, the ministry that will be his. Actually, in the temptation scene, we do not see the positive side that he chose. We see, rather, what he considered and rejected. To know what Jesus rejected is to know much about him.

Jesus never announced his mission as such. That is, he never gave a comprehensive statement of purpose on his ministry. He came as near to that statement in Luke 4 as anywhere when he identified with the saying of the prophet Isaiah and announced that the prophecy was fulfilled.

There are many understandings of the temptations. I do not believe that we must decide upon a *correct* understanding, and reject all others. Rather, as with all scripture, there may be a revealing by seeing it in a different light, by approaching it from a different angle.

Consider these perspectives on the temptations:

1. They are a literal report of the personal experience of Jesus. That is, Jesus was hungry and he thought about making bread out of rocks as he later turned water into wine. Similarly, the other temptations were what Jesus considered doing.

2. They represent symbolically the approaches to the use of power that Jesus considered. He could use his power to work miracles, to give a convincing sign, or to actually exercise political power.

3. They represent the needs, the impulses toward which all humans are drawn: the physical and fiscal side of life; the protective (if I am good, God will protect me); and, the patriotic and combative passion.

4. Dostoevsky gives major attention to the temptations in his novel, *The Brothers Karamazov*. He understands them as not simply the temptations of Jesus, but the temptations of every person. Those temptations are miracle, mystery, and authority. These, Dostoevsky says, humans typically choose instead of the God of faith.

5. Bonhoeffer calls the temptation of the stones into bread, the temptation of the *flesh*. The temptation involving the temple is the *spiritual* temptation. Finally, the kingdoms temptation is the *complete* temptation.

Read and study the passage from Luke 4:1-13 and consider possible meanings of the temptations. Relate those temptations to your own experience. Note that scripture itself is used in the dialogue of temptation—that is, scripture in debate with other scripture. Also, note that temptation did not end with that early desert scene. It continued at "an opportune time."

CONCERNING JUSTICE AND NONVIOLENCE

Secure a copy of the entire statement on "Justice and Nonviolence" found in the minutes of the 1977 Annual Conference. The statement sets forth the concern, beginning with the passage from Micah that forms the basis for the Church of the Brethren mission theme and for this book. There is then a review of the biblical view, followed by some general principles related to justice and peace, principles to guide the Church in its understanding and activity. The paper reviews a complex of problems that are illustrations of injustice and the agenda for our mission. The statement concludes with imperatives for participating with Jesus Christ in his ministry of reconciliation and redemption. We are called to such areas of involvement as peace, economic life, human rights, liberation and the stewardship of creation. The paragraphs quoted above are from the closing statement.

The congregation or the person who seriously desires to emphasize justice in the 1980's, can find a superb guiding outline in this 1977 statement.

FOR FURTHER CONSIDERATION
• Relate the temptations of Jesus to the need for a just world order. Consider, especially, the devotion of Christ to God alone, above and beyond the kingdoms of this world, even if it be one kingdom of all nations.

• How does the current violence in the world bring with it greater injustice?

• What are the conditions in which a Christian should consider a civil disobedience?

• Do you see evidence that many in the church have a higher loyalty to a political party or to the nation than to the Church?

• Are you a Christian American, or an American Christian?

SOME ACTIVITIES
Review the latest figures on the spending for military arms, worldwide and by our own nation. Study that spending in terms of its cost to the world economy, to the world's poor, and to world security.

Write a letter to your United States Representative, United States Senators and the President to express your concern about national priorities related to peace and compassion.

Study your response to the needs of people around the world, using as a guide a book such as *Christian Responsibility in a Hungry World* by Dean Freudenberger and Paul M. Minus, Jr.

Become active in some organization beyond the church which is working for world order and peace, such as the Fellowship of Reconciliation, the United Nations Association, SANE, Clergy and Laity Concerned, Women for Peace, the World Friendship Center.

Spend an evening reading with a group the T. S. Eliot play, "Murder in the Cathedral." Note and reflect upon the justifications which the knights offer for their violence.

RESOURCES FOR ADDITIONAL STUDY
Berdyaev, Nicholas. *The Realm of the Spirit and the Realm of Caesar*. Westport, Conn.: Greenwood, 1975.

Edwards, George R. *Jesus and the Politics of Violence*. New York: Harper-Row, 1972.

Eller, Vernard. *King Jesus! Manual of Arms for the Armless.* Nashville: Abingdon, 1973.

Ellul, Jacques. *Violence.* Somers, Conn.: Seabury, 1969.

Freudenberger, Dean and Minus, Paul M., Jr. *Christian Responsibility in a Hungry World.* Nashville: Abingdon, 1976.

May, Rollo. *Power and Innocence.* New York: Dell, 1976.

Ruether, Rosemary Radford. *The Radical Kingdom.* Ramsey, N.J.: Paulist Press, 1975.

Sider, Ronald. *Christ and Violence.* Scottdale, Pa.: Herald Press, 1979.

_____. *Rich Christians in an Age of Hunger.* Downers Grove, Ill.: Inter-Varsity, 1977.

Yoder, John Howard. *The Politics of Jesus.* Grand Rapids: Eerdmans, 1972.

To love tenderly
   by sharing the good news of Jesus Christ through proclamation and example.

4 WITNESS AS LIFE

*The aim of evangelization is . . .
a radical reorientation of the life,
including slavery to the world
and its powers on the one hand,
and integration into God's purpose of placing all things under
the rule of Christ on the other.*
                    RENE PADILLA

While the people pressed upon him to hear the word of God, he was standing by the Lake of Gennesaret. And he saw two boats by the lake; but the fishermen had gone out of them and were washing their nets. Getting into one of the boats, which was Simon's, he asked him to put out a little from the land. And he sat down and taught the people from the boat. And when he had ceased speaking, he said to Simon, "Put out into the deep and let down your nets for a catch." And Simon answered, "Master, we toiled all night and took nothing! But at your word I will let down the nets." And when they had done this, they enclosed a great shoal of fish; and as their nets were breaking, they beckoned to their partners in the other boat to come and help them. And they came and filled both the boats, so that they began to sink. But when Simon Peter saw it, he fell down at Jesus' knees, saying "Depart from me, for I am a sinful man, O Lord." For he was astonished, and all that were with him, at the catch of fish which they had taken; and so also were James and John, sons of Zebedee, who were partners with Simon. And Jesus said to Simon, "Do not be afraid; henceforth you will be catching men." And when they had brought their boats to land, they left everything and followed him.

Luke 5:1-11

Now the eleven disciples went to Galilee, to the mountain to which Jesus had directed them. And when they saw him they worshiped him; but some doubted. And Jesus came and said to them, "All authority in heaven and on earth has been given to me. Go therefore and make disciples of all nations, baptizing them in the name of the Father and of the Son and of the Holy Spirit, teaching them to observe all that I have commanded you; and lo, I am with you always, to the close of the age."

Matthew 28:16-20

LET OUR EVANGELISM BE FORTHRIGHT IN ITS PROCLAMATION. Christians have too often been tongue-tied, hesitant or apologetic when they have had natural opportunities to tell the good news of God. Or because they regard themselves as unworthy, their witness has been weakened by the sound of an uncertain trumpet. But our confidence is not in ourselves; it is in Christ whose example and teachings, whose life and death still speak with authority to the hearts of men, even those who seem least likely to make a profession of faith. If we experience the love of Christ, like Peter and John, "we cannot but speak of what we have seen and heard."

LET OUR EVANGELISM BE INCARNATED IN PERSONS. The good news must be communicated by individuals who are themselves the good news. One stranger can say to another, "God loves you," but the full meaning of that affirmation will be felt only when the speaker cares enough to say, "I love you." The love and concern that God feels for human beings must become incarnate in persons who will risk danger, endure suffering, and give generously of themselves on behalf of others. Without this dimension the full impact of Jesus' sacrificial death on the cross will not be understood. The best evangelists are those who today, for the sake of persons, bear in their own bodies "the marks of Jesus."

LET OUR EVANGELISM BE INCORPORATED IN ACTIONS. Through deeds of service, through evidences of personal concern, and through programs and policies that enable persons to become whole and fully human, the gospel is communicated and authenticated. The good Samaritan and the evangelist are not different persons. Individuals and congregations cannot divorce what they do from what they say. By taking a stand when basic issues are at stake; by rendering service when it may be unpopular to express concern for the oppressed; by challenging evil systems that demean and destroy human personality; by creating a caring community — in ways such as these the good news is translated into a language of deeds that everyone can understand.

> 1972 Church of the Brethren Annual Conference
> *Statement on Evangelism*

I HAVE BEEN TOLD that Rufus Bucher was asked at one time if he were a Christian. And the report is that Bucher's reply was, "Ask my wife."

It is a certain way to know (if one has a wife). There is a public self that is known along Bonita Avenue or Dundee Avenue. And there is a private self that cannot be known from the street. What a person deeply believes surely cannot be hidden from those who share the intimacies of bedroom and kitchen, the tensions of the checkbook and the raising of children. A man may boast to a stranger of his belief, but his wife knows the degree of validity in the boast. A woman may put off a question of her faith with a quick, casual answer, but her husband sees beyond that short-circuit. Sometimes, instead of answering directly, it is best to let others make their assessment of you. So, Jesus, confronted by Pilate's question, "Are you the King of the Jews?" makes no claim. He slants his reply to Pilate, "You have said so." Yes, it is true that others may be called upon to speak for us when our testimony is needed.

It may be a part of the character of the Brethren that we do not put much stock in words when it comes to witnessing to our faith. We have generally not been the street preachers, the popular evangelists, the enthusiasts whose testimonies move people to tears and repentance, to shouting and laughter. We are a quiet people. Even withdrawn. When the Brethren have been asked, "Why?" there has been a typical answer, "I let my life be my witness!" That is, "I will live the kind of life, I will embody the kind of spirit, that my neighbors can see. I will not just tell about it, I will live it." We would nod when Edgar A. Guest says, "The best of all preachers are the men who live their creeds."

The Church of the Brethren began in a time when there was a giant credibility gap in the church. With trends in the church that were corrupt, with clergy who were lazy, immoral, and unconcerned for their people, with the Church lacking any recognized standards of behavior for its members, the Church of the 17th century had a chasm between the life exemplified by Jesus Christ and the life exemplified by the members of the Body of Christ.

So, under threat of persecution, the Brethren began at Schwarzenau with a strong emphasis upon integrity. They were convinced by the Lutheran, Spener, that Christianity must be seriously practiced in daily life. Indeed, it was Spener who gave leadership to the Pietist movement, reflecting in everyday life what is claimed as a belief. "Piety" and "pious" are terms that have come to be hated. If you want to insult someone, a sure way is to say, "Oh, she is so pious." But the word has lost its root, for piety and integrity are very close in meaning. Yet, one is acceptable, the other not. The Brethren emphasized piety and integrity. They wanted more than the words of a creed; they wanted to see evidence in living that the Gospel did make a difference. Later, it came to be said, "A Dunker's word is as good as his bond." And with members of the church many business transactions were completed by a spoken word. There were no legal documents, no signatures. If a Dunker's word was given, that was all that was needed. If death came, the family would fulfill what was promised. The way the Dunkers lived was witness to their faith.

For the Brethren who were "separate from the world" in wearing the plain clothes, their very dress was a silent witness to their faith.

Through our history, we have been suspicious of those who make an exhibition of their testimony. The most vocal ones seem ostentatious to us; we hold our ground regardless of the thousands that may flock to them. Today's television evangelists seem to sell Jesus as if he were a can of beer, and reports of the wealth and lifestyles of such evangelists are not reassuring. When a person talks too quickly, too easily, too glibly, we wonder at the depth of faith there may be. We share with Sinclair Lewis a suspicion of the Elmer Gantrys. I believe that for most Brethren, the Gospel does not lie "Foursquare" with Aimee Semple

McPherson. Recently, I was talking with a man about a contemporary Elmer Gantry, known to both of us, whose private life is vastly different from his public image. The other man was aware of that discrepancy (or lack of piety). But, he said of him, "He is a great communicator of the Gospel!" But in the secret places of my mind, I asked, "How? What does he communicate?"

The Sermon on the Mount tries to be clear that faith is not recognized for its much speaking: "Not everyone who says to me, 'Lord, Lord,' shall enter the kingdom of heaven, but he who does the will of my Father who is in heaven" (Matthew 7:21, 22). And John's first epistle says, "Let us not love in word or speech, but in deed and in truth" (1 John 3:18). So we are inclined to let our lives be our witness. If the options in declaring the good news of Jesus Christ were simply proclamation and example, the Brethren have clearly chosen the latter. We are more known for our activity than for either our oral or our written testimony.

But we cannot let it rest with that. *We may take satisfaction in integrity but not in silence of proclamation. While the former may be our strength, the latter may be the crack in our structure that has been there from the beginning, has gradually widened, and if not covered or bridged, will mean our falling.*

It is not enough to let someone else give their testimony about you or for you. In fairness to Rufus Bucher, let it be said that he did not always refer people to his wife concerning his commitment. In fact, he is listed among those who became effective evangelists. It is not enough to simply depend upon your neighbor's observation of you.

What are the limitations of letting your life be your only witness? There is a kind of arrogance and presumption in such a position. It presumes that one can live such an exemplary life that everyone around will just automatically know that one is a Spirit-filled Christian.

To just let your life be your witness raises the question, "Witness to what?" Often, the person who takes such a position means that the neighbor will know that the person is honest and clean and likable, not subversive and not weird. And it is true that a neighbor can gain some impressions of these things. But that is not an indication of relationship to Jesus Christ. People can be moral and honest and friendly and have no relationship with Christ or the Church. The Christian embodies and moves with a mission that is pointed beyond these qualities. Surely morality and honesty and friendship are among the results, but there is something beyond to which the Church is pointed. The Church lives as the Body of Christ, having to do with meaning and purpose and fellowship. A person can be moral and yet be a vegetable so far as meaning in life is concerned. A person can be honest, not a thief, nor a rapist, nor a murderer, and still have no sense of purpose. A person can be clean and an acceptable neighbor, but alone, knowing neither who made him or her, nor who shares that humanity.

Without the spoken word, there can be no explicit witness to what we have experienced of God. Without the spoken word there can be no explicit witness to the meaning that Jesus Christ brings to our lives. Without the spoken word, there can be no explicit witness to what other Christians mean to us. The only way these matters can be communicated is in words. Deeds can reflect them, but they cannot make the witness complete.

Another problem in saying that my life is my witness so that I do not need to speak of my faith, is that it separates artificially the activity of speech from the rest of life. We say, "Oh, they talk and talk and never *do* anything." Or, we say, "Talk is cheap." But, taken in perspective, talking is doing, and it is not cheap. In fact, speaking is probably the most vital and pervasive of human activities. It is what separates us from other animals. And it does matter what is said. When an angel spoke to Abraham as he was ready to plunge the knife in sacrificing his son, it made a difference in Abraham's and Isaac's life (Genesis 22). When Jesus engaged the Pharisees in debate, their arguments were not just so many words. From that speaking, we have perspective on the relationship between what we inherit in our faith and the new revelation that comes. From that speaking we learn what it means to be neighbor. It means to act like a certain Samaritan.

Candidates for public office illustrate the importance of the spoken word. If they speak words that capture the imagination of a large part of the public, then their chances of being elected are greatly enhanced. If, on the other hand, they speak on foreign policy in a way that leaves people feeling uneasy and threatened, that will cost votes. Ethnic slurs may win votes from some, but will cost votes with others. Certainly, what a politician says *is* what he or she does.

Speaking is one of the most important activities of life. Truly, if *you let your life be your witness, then your faith will be spoken.*

I am convinced that if faith matures, if it has substance, it must be spoken. Speaking is the breaking forth of the bud of faith into the flower of faith. Faith will remain closed and immature until it can grow in the telling. Writing in *Liberal Christianity at the Crossroads,* John B. Cobb, Jr. says our telling the Gospel and our own faith pilgrimage is something which affects our own destiny. "If we can uncover and articulate our own inchoate story we can both be more critical of the judgments we pass upon others and more effective as participants in history. Perhaps we can learn to tell that story with conviction, in spite of our acknowledgment that it is too fragmentary and selective." There is something in the very process of having to put into words what we have felt, what we have experienced, what has been revealed to us, that transforms what has been and what is. There is a new creation. In the very telling, something is added.

The mature faith is not merely held inward as a sacred, private possession. It may begin with a vision in aloneness, upon some Mount of Transfiguration (Luke 9:28-36), or in some dark, sleepless night when "the wind blows where it wills, and you hear the sound of it, but you do not know whence it comes or whither it goes" (John 3:8). It may begin in reading from a prophet, an evangelist, or a tentmaker. It may begin with a prayer in a closet, with the door shut, and said in secret (Matthew 6:6). It may begin in worship, feeling high and lifted up (Isaiah 6:1). But mature faith does not end with such geography, such posture. Mature faith moves out with the seventy, going to every town and place where Jesus himself might come (Luke 10:1-20). It holds a commission to make disciples, to baptize, and to teach (Matthew 28:19, 20). And it feels a special urgency to proclaim, to tell what God has done in Christ Jesus: "We cannot but speak of what we have seen and heard" (Acts 4:20).

The philosopher Marcel adds a note of urgency and even of warning to the matter of declaring our faith. He said, "I am obliged to bear witness because I hold, as it were, a particle of light, and to keep it to myself would be equivalent to extinguishing it."

Rather than, "My life is my witness," it is more accurate for the Christian to say, "My witness is my life."

CONCERNING THE LUKAN TEXT

Here in Luke's Gospel we can see the beginnings of the calling of the Twelve. The context for that call is the preaching which Jesus himself was doing. He was by the lakeside where there was a crowd and where there was activity. Fishing was an important commercial activity in Palestine in that time. And it is significant that Jesus was in this place of commerce.

The story of the calling of Peter, James and John has several elements that could become symbolic suggestions.

There is a sterility in life until Jesus comes. That is, the fishermen toiled all night and caught nothing. The problem was not a lack of effort. The fishermen had exhausted themselves in their efforts. But, there was a missing ingredient. Jesus supplies what was missing.

The message is declared from the center of activity. While worship may usually be in the sanctuary, the message of Jesus was being declared where a crowd could hear and from a boat, not only a means of transportation, but also the tool of the livelihood of the fishermen.

"Put out into the deep!" Nothing happens as long as we remain near the shore and in shallow water. We are called in our faith to go out into the deep. It is there that the "catch" for the soul becomes abundant and overflowing.

So great is God's blessing, that others are needed to realize that blessing. The fish are too many to take alone. God's full blessing cannot

be realized in the solitary. It requires others to join us as a part of our common endeavor if we are to realize the fullness that God intends for us. If we try to take it in alone, we sink.

Once we have received God's gift of life, awareness dawns. Simon Peter made confession. He was uncomfortable in the presence of the Holy. By acknowledging his condition, Peter opens the way to being called by Jesus.

Jesus gives reaching other persons a priority over the commercial enterprise. This is no universal call for all to leave the labors of commerce. Rather, it was a call to the three, and it carried a promise that "fishing" for other persons would hold more meaning and satisfaction than their work with the nets. They were called not to be mere followers, but, more important, to be "fishers" in the kingdom.

Following Jesus means leaving everything and going where he leads. It meant that for three fishermen. It is not certain from the text, but we may speculate that these men had known Jesus previously. There was some basis beyond the miracle of the fish that led the men to walk away from their boats to join a ministry that would transform the world. That is a radical calling, both then and now.

CONCERNING THE MATTHEW TEXT

It has been called "The Great Commission." It has been the rallying cry for missionaries and evangelists and has provided the vision for those who have carried the Gospel throughout the world. The passage has served also to suggest the pattern of the Christian mission assignment: making disciples, baptizing, teaching them to observe Christ's commandments. The Brethren have seen it also containing a baptismal formula—that is, those who are made disciples are to be baptized three times (trine immersion) "in the name of the Father and of the Son and of the Holy Spirit."

It is a post-resurrection scene, the last appearance of Jesus to the disciples. There are two responses: worship and doubt. It is not suggested that doubt is the absence of faith. Indeed, faith implies the possibility of doubt. For all who doubt, it is clear that they have predecessors among the twelve, especially in the person of Thomas. Yet, there is a tradition that Thomas carried the Great Commission as far east as India.

To grant a commission, there must be authority. Jesus claims that authority. He speaks of having been given *all* authority in heaven and on earth. In that claim is the summation, the completeness of Christ's work.

It is not simply all individuals to whom the disciples are sent. They are to make disciples "of all nations." We have a corporate assignment. The proclamation of the good news is to go to the structures of this world.

The commission is not a dispassionate one. That is, it is not a matter of telling the story and then being unconcerned about the response. The commission is to "make disciples."

Baptism celebrates what has happened in becoming a disciple, reinforcing the decision and preparing the person for being a disciple. The Minister's Manual for the Church of the Brethren identifies these meanings of baptism:

1. An act of obedience to the teaching and example of Jesus Christ
2. A symbol of cleansing and new life
3. A sign of the covenant relationship with God
4. An initiation rite into the Body of Christ, the Church
5. An ordination into ministry
6. The beginning of a pilgrimage

Small wonder that the church which began with an illegal baptism in the Eder at Schwarzenau in 1708, has continued to find baptism one of the most significant of our rituals.

By the sequence offered, the Great Commission suggests that we are not to wait for baptism until we feel worthy or until we know all about the Christian way. We are to "count the cost" (Luke 14:26-31), make the commitment, and then begin to learn all that Jesus has commanded. The teaching and the learning are a never-ending process.

There is a promise, an assurance. There is to be a presence with us through everything. Christ will accompany us, sharing the difficulties of the road and giving us encouragement.

Concerning Evangelism

The statement from Annual Conference comes in strong, bold terms. It rebukes our failure to evangelize and our failure to trust in Christ to show us the way.

Going beyond proclamation, the statement calls for evangelism to be embodied or "incarnated" in the person of the believer, and to be expressed in everyday life, by giving service, by doing justice, and by being in a loving fellowship.

For Further Consideration

• Is it possible that you are more aware of the kind of evangelism you reject than the kind of evangelism to which you can give yourself?

• What forms of proclamation are most consistent with the Brethren character?

• Is evangelism the task of every member, or is it the task only of those who have special gifts to be evangelists?

• The Church of the Brethren membership in 1960 was about 200,000. Two decades later, there are about 25,000 fewer members. In your opinion, why has the church failed to grow in a time of general population growth? Is this something that concerns you?

• In what areas of the church's proclamation today are we in greater need of example?

SOME ACTIVITIES

Make a graph of the membership of your congregation from the time of its beginning. What does the graph picture to you?

Prepare a report on church extension in your district and for the entire denomination.

Plan a twelve-week study/action course on church growth, utilizing *Invitation to Adventure,* study materials prepared by Wayne Zunkel and Irven Stern and available from the Church of the Brethren General Board.

Write the story of your own faith pilgrimage and share it with at least one other person.

RESOURCES FOR ADDITIONAL STUDY

Cobb, John B., Jr. *Liberal Christianity at the Crossroads.* Crawfordsville, Ind.: Westminster, 1973.

Groff, Warren F. *Story Time.* Elgin: Brethren Press, 1974.

Kelley, Dean. *Why Conservative Churches Are Growing.* New York: Harper-Row, 1972.

Robinson, Paul M. (Ed.). *Call the Witnesses.* Elgin: Brethren Press, 1974.

Trueblood, Elton. *The Company of the Committed.* New York: Harper-Row, 1961.

To love tenderly
by living at one with God, at
peace with one's self, one's
family, one's neighbor, and
one's environment.

5 THE PEACE
OF
WILDNESS

Lord, we have found our friend again, but it is sick,
    wounded and exhausted.
You gave it to us once, and we took it into our hands
    when it was unspoiled,
    savage,
    but able to be tamed.
Some of us betrayed it to the "developers"
    who forced it to prostitute itself,
    so that they might take their unbridled pleasure
    from it.
And now, disfigured and contaminated,
    the earth sickens us when we draw near.

MICHAEL QUOIST

In the beginning, God created the heavens and the earth. The earth was without form and void, and darkness was upon the face of the deep; and the Spirit of God was moving over the face of the waters . . .

Then God said, "Let us make man in our image, after our likeness; and let them have dominion over the fish of the sea, and over the birds of the air, and over the cattle, and over all the earth, and over every creeping thing that creeps upon the earth." So God created man in his own image, in the image of God he created him; male and female he created them. And God blessed them, and God said to them, "Be fruitful and multiply, and fill the earth and subdue it; and have dominion over the fish of the sea and over the birds of the air and over every living thing that moves upon the earth." And God said, "Behold, I have given you every plant yielding seed which is upon the face of all the earth, and every tree with seed in its fruit; you shall have them for food. And to every beast of the earth, and to every bird of the air, and to everything that creeps on the earth, everything that has the breath of life, I have given every green plant for food." And it was so. And God saw everything that he had made, and behold, it was very good. And there was evening and there was morning, a sixth day.

Genesis 1:1, 2, 26-31

"You shall love the Lord your God with all your heart, and with all your soul, and with all your strength, and with all your mind; and your neighbor as yourself."   Luke 10:27

Christian community witnesses to the character of life. At the heart of this relationship is a God-given love for one another and ourselves. This love reflects an unwavering care and trust for one another and requires a continuing self-giving to the other. This love is exemplified by Christ who gave everything for us. Growth comes when we have the security of knowing that we are unconditionally loved by another. When our relationship is bound by Christ, we feel accepted, loved and cared for. Love promotes growth.

Jesus' life thrust was toward growth; he looked at people in terms of what they could become. Growth experiences are needed today in our inner lives, our marriages, our churches, and our world. Jesus said his purpose in coming was to enable us to find life "in all its fullness."

John 10:10 NEB

Our relationships can be authentic only when we honestly and openly share with one another our true thoughts and feelings. We have been called to speak the truth in love. There is a risk in personal honesty and in openly facing our own faults and feelings; when we begin to see and acknowledge our own shortcomings, we likewise become more accepting of others. At that point, we can truly begin a relationship freed from the barriers of mistrust and deception. Our relationships can then be rooted in the wholeness and perfection that Christ has brought to us.

We become free by knowing that Christ is alive within us and by choosing and receiving this bond of togetherness. For the Christian, authentic relationship has its roots in Christ. True freedom comes in the recognition of our relationship to God and our interdependence on each other. Freedom is accepting who we are, and whose we are in Christ.

1977 Church of the Brethren Annual Conference
Marriage and Divorce

I N THE MID-1960's, there came to Northern Illinois an ice storm, chilling with its clutch, devastating in its damage. On a winter afternoon, the quiet, slow, cold rain began. The upper air was warmer than the earth's surface, which was covered with a thin blanket of snow, just below freezing. The rain began its earthward journey as liquid, but as it touched an earthly object, it cemented itself to what was already there. Soon the freezing rain covered our world with danger. The glazed sidewalks threatened those who tried to walk along them. The little-traveled streets were rapidly covered with sheets of ice; only the foolish would try to drive there. Power lines and trees were surrounded by the rain and then ice, accumulating weight, and then snapping and falling to the ground. With large limbs often falling on telephone and electric wires, the services of those wires were soon cut to the entire city.

Without telephones, without travel, without electricity, with temperatures dropping to around zero, it was a dangerous and frightening time. There was the further hazard of trees falling on our house. We wondered how long we could maintain reasonable warmth in the house. Those neighbors with gas stoves were fortunate; they turned on the ovens, opened the oven doors and heated the kitchen. Unfortunately, our kitchen range was electric. The furnace was gas, but depended upon an electric fan to send the heat.

It was four days before electric service was restored to our city. Strangely, those four days are remembered as a time of closeness with neighbors and family. With no television or radio, we discovered each other in a new way. We talked and played games and enjoyed an apprehensive quiet. In that quiet, we felt the presence of God's Spirit with us. We learned to know our neighbors better and we worked together to contribute to each other's safety and comfort. Love found expression through a greater intimacy and a reaching out to the neighbor. And the Spirit found a way to gather us together and draw us toward itself.

Such a winter episode is a part of the wildness of life that paradoxically brings our peace. In that wildness is felt the Creator; by experiencing the Creator, we are much more in tune with creation. Henry David Thoreau wrote with unique understanding of our relationship to nature. He said that "in Wildness is the preservation of the World. Every tree sends its fibers forth in search of the Wild. The cities import it at any price. Men plow and sail for it. From the forest and wilderness come the tonics and barks which brace mankind." In *Walden,* Thoreau develops that theme as a way of pointing toward what I would identify as the transcendence of God.

> We need the tonic of wildness,—to wade sometimes in marshes where the bittern and the meadow-hen lurk, and hear the booming of the snipe; to smell the whispering sedge where only some wilder and more solitary fowl builds her nest, and the mink crawls with its belly close to the ground. At the same time that we are earnest to explore and learn all things, we require that all things be mysterious and unexplorable, that land and sea be infinitely wild, unsurveyed and unfathomed by us because unfathomable. We can never get enough of nature . . . We need to witness our own limits transgressed.

We attain peace with our universe as we experience the wildness of life.

When Jesus was tested on the direction of his vocation (Luke 4:1-13); when Jesus was overwhelmed by the presence of people (Luke 5:16); when Jesus was in despair in the face of the cross (Mark 14:26-42), he went to the place of the *wild*, the wilderness. It was there that Jesus was restored, was given direction, was delivered from the devil for a time. It was in the wilderness that Jesus reordered his life and found peace.

That is more than the story of Jesus. It is universal that in the place of wildness, where we are with "wild beasts," precisely there, the angels will minister to us as they did to Jesus.

The wild poses a challenge to the human family. We have the urge to tame. We turn the buffalo grass into nice bermuda lawns and concrete slabs. We transform the young, defiant stallion into an obedient saddle horse. The problem with taming is that it easily becomes the drive to control. Even in human life we feel the urge to tame and control. The story of *One Flew Over the Cuckoo's Nest* is of a wild man and the efforts to tame him. His taming was finally achieved when he was given a lobotomy. The patient, however, had a friend, who thought him better dead than without his characteristic wildness, and the friend introduced the patient to death.

We often feel ourselves in a contest with the wild: the human against the elements of nature. There are those environmentalists who contend that the ecological crisis is upon us because of the Judeo-Christian world view. These critics of our faith say that we believe in human dominance over nature and the natural environment. They quote our scripture from Genesis and say that in human "dominion over the fish of the sea, and over the birds of the air, and over the cattle, and over all the earth, and over every creeping thing that creeps upon the earth" (Genesis 1:26), there is established a relationship that rapes other forms of life. In domination, we have created a science and a technology that has despoiled our natural environment. Certainly, our behavior in relation to the environment through history can easily be criticized. We have sinned and must make confession. But having "dominion" was never meant to imply that Jews and Christians could do as they please with the rest of nature. Scripture is interwoven with injunctions on behalf of the earth and on behalf of other forms of life.

To have dominion is in contrast with owning. Precisely, the natural order is not given to us as a private possession. To have dominion is to have a stewardship rather than an ownership. As humans, we are not outside of creation; we are within it. True, the human species has a unique status, a unique role. But we are as much a part of nature as rocks and rabbits. John B. Cobb has said that "the absolutization of human life at the total expense of sub-human life seems to lead to a mode of being in which human existence itself would be sub-human in quality." (Quoted in *Christian Century*, December 1, 1971, "The Ecological Challenge to Christian Ethics" by James C. Livingston.) If we do not understand ourselves to be a part of the natural, even the wild, we are not in a proper relationship with the whole of creation.

The late British economist, E. F. Schumacher, wrote a book with the intriguing title, *Small Is Beautiful: Economics as if People Mattered*. In that volume, he says that "one of the most fateful errors of our age is the belief that the problem of production has been solved . . . Mankind has at last come of age." Schumacher reflects upon the origin and the shape of the error.

> Modern man does not experience himself as a part of nature but as an outside force destined to dominate and conquer it. He even talks of a battle with nature, forgetting that, if he won the battle, he would find himself on the losing side. Until quite recently, the battle seemed to go well enough to give him the illusion of unlimited powers, but not so well as to bring the possibility of total victory into view."

Schumacher believes that we approach the problem trying to construct a political system so perfect that wickedness disappears. It is widely held that everybody is born good—if they become bad, the system did it. So we seek ways of manipulating and managing not only the natural order, but also human nature.

What a challenge that is! To gain power over everything! Why, it's like being God, but not the God of our Lord Jesus Christ. That God exercises power in weakness and freedom. There is a wildness, an uncontrolled part of life, which God has not put under his thumb, and which, interestingly, even bears witness to God.

We are called to feel ourselves a part of the wild, of nature, and to live in relation to the rest of creation. There is more peace for us when we are vulnerable to the rest of creation than when we feel in total control of ourselves and of our environment. Again, going back to Thoreau: "We need the tonic of wildness . . . We need to witness our own limits transgressed."

CONCERNING THE GENESIS TEXT

Our Holy Scripture opens in grand and sweeping style. As has often been noted, there is here no argument for the existence of God. God is simply affirmed. God is the foundation of all life. The first chapter of Genesis is such a marvelous faith statement and affirmation that it is tragedy that there are those who would trivialize it by making it literalistic science.

Read the entire first chapter of Genesis, and then compare the story of creation with the story of creation that is found in Genesis 2. In the first story, for example, God creates the human species in God's own image—"male and female he created them." In the second story, man is created and later woman is created from the rib of man. The order of creation is also different in the two stories. Do you find any particular meaning in the differences?

Consider the last part of Genesis 1. What do the verses 26-31 suggest about relationships within creation? Discuss the meaning of "dominion."

CONCERNING THE LUKAN TEXT

A lawyer rises to challenge Jesus with a question whose modern paraphrase is "What must I do to be saved?" (Luke 10:25-28). As he did frequently, Jesus responded to question with a question. "What is the summation, what is the essence of your religious teaching?" The lawyer responded, saying that the heart of the religious teaching is the love of God and the love of neighbor. In his answer, the lawyer combines Deuteronomy 6:4, "Hear, O Israel: The Lord our God is one Lord; and you shall love the Lord your God with all your heart, and with all your soul, and with all your might," which every faithful Jew would repeat daily, with Leviticus 19:18, "You shall love your neighbor as yourself." You have replied well, Jesus told the lawyer, live your reply and you will be "saved."

What follows the principle of loving God and loving neighbor as the summation of the religious teaching, is a good example of how very simple teachings become complex in their application. The lawyer then poses the question, "But, who is my neighbor?" and the response is the parable of the Good Samaritan. The lawyer might have asked, "But, what does it mean to love God with all my heart, soul, strength, and mind, when I have responsibility for a family and to my employer?"

As you consider the text from Luke, think about the different forms of loving God: heart, soul, strength, mind. Is there significance in the order of love, that is, that one loves God before loving neighbor? Does this passage suggest that our being at one with God leads to peace with our universe?

CONCERNING OUR RELATIONSHIPS

The 1977 Annual Conference Statement on Marriage and Divorce begins with affirmations about "Relationship in the Faith Community." Only when that context is established for consideration, does the statement move to look at marriage and divorce and remarriage. The statement identifies God as the source of love for ourselves and for others. The statement contends that we grow when we have the security of knowing that we are unconditionally loved by another. There is an implied need for growth in relationships. Authentic relationship is possible only when we accept the risk of being honest and open. Note the statement about freedom. What do you understand it means to "become free"?

Secure a copy of the entire statement to study the counsel of the Church on what it means to fulfill God's intention within marriage.

FOR FURTHER CONSIDERATION

• The peace we seek is not a passive peace. Despite all the emphasis upon the hazards of life stress, the aim of life is not to avoid all stress. Discuss the positive uses of stress; the difference between stress that is positive and stress that is destructive.

• The story of Noah suggests that all of created life rides with humanity on the ark toward being saved; our destinies are interwoven.

• Do you recall times and places where you have felt overwhelmed by the creation around you?

• What do our times say to you about having animal pets?

• Is it easier for you to be at peace with the environment than with your family or your neighbors?

SOME ACTIVITIES

While in study or at worship, greet those around you with the greeting of "Peace!" or "Shalom!" The Hebrew word, "Shalom," is often translated into the English word, "Peace." For the Hebrew people it implied a national security and the absence of warfare, but its meaning was larger for it conveyed, also, a state of wholeness and wellbeing in the inner lives of people and in their interpersonal relationships. It was a state in which a people could live out faithfully their covenant relationship with God. Shalom is often used as a greeting to convey the hope, the wish, for this kind of peace for the other person and for all people. Study the natural environment and ways in which you and your congregation can live at peace with the air and the water and the landscaping around you.

Ask a class member to prepare a report on family violence, its nature, its prevalence, and possible causes and treatment. Try to determine the extent to which family violence is a problem in your congregation and your community. What can your church do to minister in such situations?

Become acquainted with the activities of the Humane Society in your community.

RESOURCES FOR ADDITIONAL STUDY

Dillard, Annie. *Pilgrim at Tinker Creek*. Des Plaines, Ill.: Bantam, 1975.

Jones, Thomas A. "Toward a Planetary Ecological Ethic," *World Future Society Bulletin*, September-October, 1978.

Killinger, John. *Bread for the Wilderness, Wine for the Journey*. Waco, Texas: Word Books, 1976.

Lindbergh, Anne Morrow. *Gift from the Sea*. Westminster, Md.: Random, 1978.

Merton, Thomas. *The Seven-Story Mountain*. New York: Harcourt Brace Jovanovich, 1978.

O'Connor, Elizabeth. *Journey Inward, Journey Outward*. New York: Harper-Row, 1975.

Ruether, Rosemary Radford. "The Biblical Vision of the Ecological Crisis," *The Christian Century*, November 22, 1978.

Thomas a Kempis. *The Imitation of Christ*. Cleveland: Collins-World, 1976.

Thoreau, Henry David. *Walden*. Westminster, Md.: Modern Library, 1950.

Ward, Barbara and Dubas, Rene. *Only One Earth:* The Care and Maintenance of a Small Planet. New York: Norton, 1972.

Wilson, Leland. *Silver City*. Elgin: Brethren Press, 1980.

To love tenderly
by building community and
wholeness in all aspects of life.

6 THE SAVING COMMUNITY

*It is part of the calling of
the church to show the world
what true community means.*
SUZANNE DE DIETRICH

For by the grace given to me I bid every one among you not to think of himself more highly than he ought to think, but to think with sober judgment, each according to the measure of faith which God has assigned him. For as in one body we have many members, and all the members do not have the same function, so we, though many, are one body in Christ, and individually members one of another. Having gifts that differ according to the grace given to us, let us use them: if prophecy, in proportion to our faith; if service, in our serving; he who teaches, in his teaching; he who exhorts, in his exhortation; he who contributes, in liberality; he who gives aid, with zeal; he who does acts of mercy, with cheerfulness.

Let love be genuine; hate what is evil, hold fast to what is good; love one another with brotherly affection; outdo one another in showing honor. Never flag in zeal, be aglow with the Spirit, serve the Lord. Rejoice in your hope, be patient in tribulation, be constant in prayer. Contribute to the needs of the saints, practice hospitality.

Bless those who persecute you; bless and do not curse them. Rejoice with those who rejoice, weep with those who weep. Live in harmony with one another; do not be haughty, but associate with the lowly; never be conceited. Repay no one evil for evil, but take thought for what is noble in the sight of all. If possible, so far as it depends upon you, live peaceably with all. Beloved, never avenge yourselves, but leave it to the wrath of God; for it is written, "Vengeance is mine, I will repay, says the Lord." No, "if your enemy is hungry, feed him; if he is thirsty, give him drink; for by so doing you will heap burning coals upon his head." Do not be overcome by evil, but overcome evil with good.

Romans 12:3-21

To these early Baptists, faith which was not experienced as an inner commitment to Christ and expressed in practical acts in everyday life was an invalid faith. Only through faith-obedience, expressed voluntarily through acts of love, is one ever made whole.

For the Reformers, salvation was an objective act of God. For Mack, salvation was strongly subjective with great emphasis placed upon the centrality of love in the inner being. Love, to Mack was rooted in one's relationship with God, which flowered in loving relationships with others. The ultimate religious experience to this sensitive man was the experience of God's loving, healing, Holy Spirit manifested in love and concern for those in the community of faith and in compassion even for one's enemies. Mack's understanding of salvation was clearly Pietistic.

Mack's interpretation of faith was not only in terms of obedience, but was also like that of a growing plant rather than a finished structure. He could never accept creedal statements as definitive or systematic theologies as final. His sermons were designed to encourage his congregation in their struggle to grow in love, purity, and grace, "in favor with God and man." With other Pietists, Mack believed strongly in the Christian life as one of growth and openness. He recognized the possibility of a person's regeneration "to a considerable extent even before his baptism in water."

William G. Willoughby
Counting the Cost

A FEW YEARS AGO, in Durango, Colorado, I met and talked with a man whose statement of his relationship to the church I have not forgotten. We had been talking about the church, about my being a minister, about my being Brethren, a breed of which he had no acquaintance. Then he gave a succinct summary of his own relationship to the church.

"I'm a Methodist. Anyhow, my folks wuz Methodist. And I'm a member, only I don't belong. You know what I mean. I mean I got baptized an' all that, but I never done nuthin' about it."

That young man's comment reflects a condition that afflicts a major part of the human family. And, as with the man, it is known within the church. There are many who are members of the church but who really do not feel that they belong.

The problem may be growing. Lifestyle changes in the past decade have tended toward more individualness and less commitment to other people in a living community. Nationally, from 1971-1979, the number of unmarried couples living together more than doubled; among those under twenty-five, the number increased by a multiple of eight. In the decade of the 70's, the number of one-person households increased by 42%, and as the decade closed, half of the children of the nation relate to one parent only. Divorce became much more common during the decade, including divorce among those who had been married for many years. Had these trends not developed, had there been no single households, no unmarried cohabitation, no divorce, there would still have been the need for community. The fact that these trends are present simply intensifies the need for community.

Suzanne de Dietrich, the French theologian, says, "Our firm belief is that it is a part of the calling of the church to show the world what true community means: a fellowship of free persons bound to one another by a common calling and a common service. Only in Christ can we solve the tension between freedom and authority, between the right of the individual person to attain fulness of life and the claim of the community as a whole on each of its members. For in and through him we learn what it means to be perfectly free, yet obedient unto death; to come as a servant, yet through this very self-abasement to attain fulness of life" (Suzanne de Dietrich, *The Witnessing Community*). Here we have the ingredients of true community.

True community is not a gathering or a collection. It is a fellowship. There is a Greek word that has come to have common usage within the church, a word that means fellowship: *koinonia*. A church school class within our congregation calls itself by that title. The late Clarence Jordan, interpreter of the Cottonpatch Version of scripture, called his interracial community in Americus, Georgia, Koinonia Farms. And the term is planted generously elsewhere. Basically, koinonia means having communion with each other, sharing each with the other. There is an implied closeness, an intimacy. The Eucharist is a celebration of fellowship. "The cup of blessing which we bless, is it not a participation in the blood of Christ? The bread which we break, is it not a participation in the body of Christ?" (1 Corinthians 10:16). In the fellowship, our being "in Christ" and "with Christ" brings us to community; we belong to each other, and we are committed to each other. We are a member and we do belong.

One of the most popular interpreters of the Christian faith over the past few decades is C. S. Lewis. The Oxford professor not only wrote numerous books, but he was also a writer of letters. Several of his letters are in a book by Sheldon Vanauken, *A Severe Mercy*. The book is a love story of Vanauken and his wife, beautiful and romantic, but then tragic, as she becomes victim to a mysterious disease, and slowly her life ebbs away. It is genuine fellowship that Vanauken experienced with Lewis and with others in the time of dying. Listen as he describes the relationship. "C. S. Lewis was to be *the* friend in my loss and grief, the one hand in mine as I walked through a dark and desolate night. Other friends gave me love, and it was a fire to warm me. But Lewis was the friend I needed, the friend who would go with me down to the bedrock of meaning." This is truly koinonia, a sense of community. Within that community there are different levels of closeness, but hopefully, always one or more who will go "down to the bedrock of meaning."

To experience community requires the free choice. We are part of the fellowship, not because it is required, but because we have chosen. Great numbers of people remain outside the fellowship because, they say, "My folks forced me to go to church when I was a child." We hear people forty years old and older using that excuse. If true, they are still not free, for they are permitting the action of their parents to determine what they do.

In the community, we are free, yet bound. Freedom is never a simple, loose matter. The parable of the prodigal son is a parable of freedom. It is a parable with which we easily identify, and thus, it has become to us the most known of the parables of Jesus. The younger son wanted to break free of the restraints of home. He wanted to be free of the expectations of his father. He wanted to be free from his tedious brother. What one of us has not harbored the desire to be free from it all —free from work, free from family, free from school, free from church.

So the prodigal wants to be free, and goes his way to a far country. There he can express himself in full freedom. He can say what he likes. He can ignore customs. He can live with no expectations placed upon him. He is free even to squander his life in loose living.

But that libertine freedom takes a strange turn. A famine arose, a deep hunger, and the prodigal was in want. The kind of freedom he had was not satisfying. It was a poor, cheap bargain. So he became a hired man, a slave to another. And this man, the story says, "sent him into his fields to feed swine" (Luke 15:15). Sent him! Where now his boasted freedom? The kind of freedom he chose made him a slave. That is the tragedy of the far country; it soon enslaves us.

When the prodigal began to yearn to be once again a part of the community, he still had a struggle with freedom. Now, he was disillusioned with it all, and he wanted none. "Treat me as one of your hired servants," he would say (Luke 15:19). But the prodigal is not received back into the Father's house, the community, on that basis. He comes into the community freely choosing, but knowing that his free choice has certain implications.

Much of Paul's writing has to do with freedom and law. When Paul wrote of the law, he had reference to the Jewish teachings from scripture and from rabbinic sources that specified certain expectations. They were the requirements to be a good Jew and to belong to the community of faith. What Paul said about the law and freedom is very complex. On the one hand, in the first part of Romans 7, Paul contends that there is death to the old way of the law; the law no longer applies. The law has no binding power for those who have experienced death to the old and birth to the new. We are free! By the end of the chapter, Paul says that he agrees that the law is good, and elsewhere he speaks of the law as the teacher which comes to prepare us for the Gospel of Christ.

For our own lives, we could draw a parallel with the law. It might be the Bible; it is the term that Clarence Jordan used in updating the concept in the Cottonpatch Version of the Pauline epistles. That is, we must do something because "the Bible says . . . " Or, the law could be considered somewhat the equivalent of the sense of *should*. Under freedom, we do what we desire; under law, we do what we should.

It seems clear that Paul lived with both freedom and law; and it seems clear that the Christian who lives in community will do both what he or she wants to do, but along with that, there will be some "shoulds." Indeed, *we live in the tension between law and freedom, but in Christ, we are turned toward freedom.*

We are free persons, but bound to God, and bound to one another. That binding is the cost for community. In the material above, Suzanne de Dietrich speaks of the tension between the right of the individual person and the claim of the community on each of its members.

The claims of the community are essential to realize and maintain community. Only by its claims upon the person, its requirements for membership, can the community exist. The community requires some sense of identity. By the claims that it makes, the community shapes its identity.

The novel, *The Rabbi,* by Noah Gordon, tells of a Jewish man who meets the daughter of a Protestant minister. They are attracted, yet it seems that the religious barrier must pull them apart. He intends to be a rabbi, yet he could hardly be a Jewish rabbi and be married to this woman. He wanted her, yet he also wanted to be a rabbi. Unknown to him, she begins the process of conversion, studying with the very rabbi who trained the man she loved. When, finally, she was ready, she had her baptism, a complete immersion. As she prepared for her baptism, the old Jewish woman who helped her, told her that it was to cleanse her from all former religions so that she could pray to God really feeling like a Jew.

Could she feel like a Jew? That was a question many times after her marriage, and her most critical time was when her father, the Congregational minister, asked her to look him in the eye and tell him that she was a Jew.

It is important for the Jew to know that he or she is a Jew. I remember teaching a youth class at the Highland Avenue Church of the Brethren in Elgin several years ago. At one time, the class was discussing the faith and history of Israel. My second son had a friend who was Jewish, and we invited his mother to come and talk to the class about the Jewish Law. She told the class how she kept a kosher home. She bought her meat in Chicago. She kept special sets of dishes. It was much work and expense. Why did she do it, the class asked her. Was it to be a good person? Was it to get to heaven?

"No," she said, "I do it to remind me that I am a Jew. I need that constant reminder. Only by reminding myself can I be sure of being ready when the next great test comes. All Jews know that with the next Hitler, with the next massacre, it might be them."

There is need for identity in order for community to exist. As Brethren, we would have a greater sense of community if we established more claims (in the words of the Jewish woman, "that constant reminder") upon the person, and if we accepted those claims for our own lives.

Our binding in community is "by a common calling and a common service." The identity of the community helps to establish the calling, and it is through the community that we hear the calling. We are all called into fellowship with the Holy Spirit and with each other. It is our common service, the mission factor, which prevents the community, with its unique identity, from becoming a narrowly provincial, anti-ecumenical body. It is precisely as a strong community that we can offer the greatest service to others of the Christian faith and to the world. As Christians, we are the new Israel, inheriting the same mission as Israel: The Lord says, it is too easy a thing that you should be my servant to raise up Brethren, to be ecstatic in celebration, to be satisfied in your own community; "I will give you as a light to the nations, that my salvation may reach to the end of the earth" (Isaiah 42:6).

CONCERNING THE ROMAN TEXT

What does it require to experience true community and wholeness in the Church? Paul speaks to that question in the quoted text with three basic ideas:

1. *Relating to the community.* Understand that each of you is part of the community and valuable, not because all have the same function, but because we have complementary functions, reflecting the marvelous diversity God has given us. The obligation is to use the gifts we have—and Paul even admonishes us on the attitude with which we approach our service. We are to be cheerful, have zeal, and to practice humility.

Elizabeth O'Connor in *Eighth Day of Creation* makes a strong case for a central task of the church being that of identifying and liberating the gifts of the members. That may be one of our important tasks for the decade of the 80's.

2. *Love as the Christian norm.* Jesus said that people would know his disciples by this: "if you have love for one another" (John 13:35). It is love that enables people to work together; in the church, it is love that is the motive for serving God. Here Paul offers some characteristics of love, though not as many as in 1 Corinthians 13. Love is an emotional experience, involving affection and entering into the joys and the sorrows of the other. Paul speaks of zeal and of being aglow. But love is more than emotional. It means being in prayer, practicing hospitality, and contributing to the needs of others. There is even a note about showing honor.

3. *Love even your enemies.* The passage has echoes of the Sermon on the Mount. It identifies humility as one of the ways we are able to live in harmony when there is conflict. Avoid conceit and

haughtiness, he tells us. How many of our problems could be significantly lessened if we would but follow that advice.

It may appear that Paul is advocating a positive response to the enemy as a way of defeating the enemy. "For by so doing you will heap burning coals upon his head." Augustine referred to "the burning shame" which goodness in response to evil evokes. But Paul never intends service as a technique to overcome an adversary. Then, it would not be goodness, but would be dishonest manipulation. (Note that Paul is quoting a scripture from the Writings: Proverbs 25:21, 22.) It is not the evil person, but evil that is overcome with good.

CONCERNING ALEXANDER MACK AND COMMUNITY

The early Brethren community had a leader who believed strongly in practical expressions of faith, and of the corporate nature of that faith. Wholeness was in love and obedience, but it involved more than the individual.

William G. Willoughby, author of *Counting the Cost: The Life of Alexander Mack*, makes the point that Mack understood his faith more as something growing than as a finished creedal statement or theology. That growing begins before baptism and continues throughout life.

Elsewhere, Mack is cited as believing that an individual ethic is not capable of dealing with corporate evil. "A Christian cannot retreat into a haven of solitary peace and self-satisfaction." Mack's urgency for having a sense of community came from his own life experience.

FOR FURTHER CONSIDERATION

• Are you a member of the church, but don't really belong? What does belonging require?

• How could your congregation develop a greater sense of community?

• In the tension between the freedom of the individual person and the claims of the faith community upon that person, toward which side does your congregation give greatest weight?

• Do you feel a sense of identity as one of the Brethren?

• What does it mean to honor another person?

• Is it always possible to redeem a relationship? That is, to make a friend of your enemy? If not, how is the Christian to live with such an absence of wholeness?

SOME ACTIVITIES

In a small group, take turns in focusing upon one person and identifying the gifts of that person. Give encouragement to develop and use those gifts.

List the kinds of service you offer as a congregation. Add to the list the common service you would like to see undertaken.

Express appreciation to a friend who offers to you a genuine sense of koinonia.

RESOURCES FOR ADDITIONAL STUDY

de Dietrich, Suzanne. *The Witnessing Community*. Crawfordsville, Ind.: Westminster, 1978.

Jung, Carl. *Memories, Dreams, and Reflections*. Westminster, Md.: Random, 1965.

Keck, Robert. *The Spirit of Synergy*. Nashville: Abingdon, 1978.

O'Connor, Elizabeth. *Eighth Day of Creation*. Waco, Texas: Word Books, 1971.

Vanauken, Sheldon. *A Severe Mercy*. New York: Harper-Row, 1977.

Willoughby, William G. *Counting the Cost*. Elgin: Brethren Press, 1979.

To love tenderly
>*by confronting and caring for one another.*

7 AN ENDURING LOVE

Of all the worn, smudged,
dog's-eared words in our
vocabulary, "love" is certainly the
grubbiest, smelliest, slimiest.
Bawled from a million pulpits,
lasciviously crooned through hun-
dreds of loudspeakers, it has
become an outrage to good taste
and decent feeling, an obscenity
which one hesitates to pronounce.
And yet it has to be pronounced,
for after all, Love is the last word.
ALDOUS HUXLEY

If I speak in the tongues of men and of angels, but have not love, I am a noisy gong or a clanging cymbal. And if I have prophetic powers, and understand all mysteries and all knowledge, and if I have all faith, so as to remove mountains, but have not love, I am nothing. If I give away all I have, and if I deliver my body to be burned, but have not love, I gain nothing.

Love is patient and kind; love is not jealous or boastful; it is not arrogant or rude. Love does not insist on its own way; it is not irritable or resentful; it does not rejoice at wrong, but rejoices in the right. Love bears all things, believes all things, hopes all things, endures all things.

Love never ends; as for prophecies, they will pass away; as for tongues, they will cease; as for knowledge, it will pass away. For our knowledge is imperfect and our prophecy is imperfect; but when the perfect comes, the imperfect will pass away. When I was a child, I spoke like a child, I thought like a child, I reasoned like a child; when I became a man, I gave up childish ways. For now we see in a mirror dimly, but then face to face. Now I know in part, then I shall understand fully, even as I have been fully understood. So faith, hope, love abide, these three; but the greatest of these is love.

1 Corinthians 13

I wish to propose a theory and to make some remarks about it, arising largely out of my contacts and discussions with artists and poets. The theory is: Creativity occurs in an act of encounter and is to be understood with this encounter as its center.

Cézanne sees a tree. He sees it in a way no one else has ever seen it. He experiences, as he no doubt would have said, "being grasped by the tree." The arching grandeur of the tree, the mothering spread, the delicate balance as the tree grips the earth — all these and many more characteristics of the tree are absorbed into his perception and are felt throughout his nervous structure. These are part of the vision he experiences. This vision involves an omission of some aspects of the scene and a greater emphasis on other aspects and the ensuing rearrangement of the whole; but it is more than the sum of all these. Primarily it is a vision that is now not a tree, but Tree; the concrete tree Cézanne looked at is formed into the essence of tree. However original and unrepeatable his vision is, it is still

a vision of all trees triggered by his encounter with this par-
ticular one.

The painting that issues out of this encounter between a human
being, Cézanne, and an objective reality, the tree, is literally
new, unique and original. Something is born, comes into
being, something that did not exist before — which is as good a
definition of creativity as we can get. Thereafter everyone who
looks at the painting with intensity of awareness and lets it
speak to him or her will see the tree with the unique powerful
movement, the intimacy between the tree and the landscape,
and the architectural beauty which literally did not exist in our
relation with trees until Cézanne experienced and painted
them. I can say without exaggeration that I never really saw a
tree until I had seen and absorbed Cézanne's paintings of them.
                                        Rollo May
                                        The Courage to Create

THERE IS NO RICHER WORD in the English language than love. Rich in
its meaning to the human family, "love" covers a myriad of emotions and activities, so diverse that the term bears the burden of trivial-
ization. Listen to our uses of the word love:

"That kid loves Dr. Pepper! He drinks it all the time."

"Let's get out the old Bing Crosby records. I just love those mellow
tones."

"Do you feel like making love?"

"I cannot stand her leadership. But when you talk about getting her
out of office, I have to ask myself what is the loving thing to do?"

"How can you say that you love your child when you just take off
and leave the family?"

These are everyday uses of the word love. The Greek language
through which the original New Testament comes to us was more pre-
cise in this aspect of language. The Greeks had four words which we
translate into love. For emotional passion and desire, they used the
word *eros*. For steadfast affection that binds people together, even
when passion is spent, they used the word *philia*. For the feelings of
child for parent, a brother for sister, a parent for child, in which sex is
not a part, they used the word *storge*. For that attitude of goodwill that
cannot be altered, for the desire for human good that nothing can kill,
they used the word *agape*. The New Testament associated *agape* with
God.

Agape love means to seek the good of those who are within our
range of influence, whatever their attitude toward us. They may not like
us. They may tell lies about us. They may see the ambiguity in our
character and exploit it. We may not like them. We may not like the

sound of their voice. We may not like the way they whine and complain. We may not like the way they are arrogant and try to show their superiority. All of those feelings are irrelevant to agape love. Agape love is the willingness to act for the other person's interest when you want to and when you do not want to. Agape love is the ability to get beyond the immediate chemistry of personal interaction, and to act on behalf of the other.

But love in the Christian faith does not end with agape. All of the loves of the Greek terms are a part of our wholeness. We need them all; all are expressions of our humanity and are needed to complete God's purpose in us.

Love is the beginning and the fulfillment of the Christian faith. Love is the essence of God (1 John 4:16). By love will all be known who follow the way of Jesus (John 13:35). That is not only a scriptural perspective and a personal affirmation from within the faith, it is how Christianity can be understood from the outside. Gandhi of India, for example, understood our faith in that way. Gandhi was not a Christian, but lived out the ideal of love far more than most Christians, to such an extent that many Christians have been puzzled at how someone could be so loving if not a Christian. Many even try to make him a Christian. But trying to baptize Gandhi's ashes will only make a mess. He was not a Christian, but knew Christianity. He had this advice to give Christians with regard to the nation of India:

> I would suggest, first, that all of you Christians, missionaries and all, begin to live more like Jesus Christ . . .

> I would suggest that you must practice your religion without adulterating or toning it down . . .

> Third, I would suggest that you must put your emphasis upon love, for *love is the center and soul of Christianity.*

> . . . Fourth, I would suggest that you study the non-Christian religions and culture more sympathetically in order to find the good that is in them, so that you might have a more sympathetic approach to people.
>
> E. Stanley Jones, *The Christ of the Indian Road*
> Italics added

Listen to that remarkable assessment by Gandhi: love is the center and soul of Christianity. Not doctrine. Not creed. Not ritual. Not learning. Not the church. Except as these are expressions of love.

Love. I fear I know little about it. And I am impressed that those who talk the most about love and caring are often the very persons from whom I feel the least love. There is a magnitude to love, a mystery in love that simply overwhelms me. I sense there are some principles involved in love, and it is to some of those principles that we now turn.

We are not free to love until we have felt loved. Yet, we cannot go out and seek or demand that others love us. It is when we have really been loved and felt loved by another person that we can love others.

There are times when we can feel that no one loves us. And even when love comes to us, we can turn it away. Anthony Quinn, the movie actor who portrayed the sensual and tempestuous Zorba the Greek, tells of concern about love in his own life struggle. He talks of a man who was capable of loving but could never receive love. And then, Anthony Quinn, in his autobiography, *The Original Sin,* makes this declaration, "The inability to accept love is to me the original sin, sadder than all others." There is, indeed, something defeating, something devastating, in extending love, but having it unreceived. The beginning point of loving is being open to receive love.

We are not free to love until we have received love; yet, if it does not come from others, we cannot seek or demand that others love us. C. S. Lewis in *The Four Loves* writes of "those pathetic people who simply want friends and can never make any. The very condition of having friends is that we should want something else besides friends." If we seek love directly, we will never find it. In my own wedding and in many of the weddings at which I have officiated, there has been incorporated those lines from St. Exupery:

> Love does not consist in gazing at each other
> but in looking outward together in the same
> direction.

We are not free to love until we have felt loved and have a healthy self-love. That is some of the meaning in the teaching, "You shall love your neighbor as yourself" (Mark 12:31). You are prepared for loving neighbor by loving yourself—not in the terms of an egotist, but a genuine sense of self-worth and self-affirmation.

Now, I know that I am drawn to some persons and repelled from some persons for reasons that are unknown. There is a mystery in human chemistry. Usually, there is a mutuality in relationships. Both parties are either attracted or repelled, the reasons for which can be only partially surmised. Not always. Sometimes a person wants to be very close to us and we do not share that desire. Sometimes we are attracted to a person, but they, not to us. These are honest, human feelings. And love is involved. But love is involved, also, when we can act on behalf of the other person beyond the feeling level. It is possible for us to act for a person, to support a person, to express caring, even when we do not easily relate on a personal basis. That is one way in which the Church is different from being simply a group of friends. The Church calls us to care about those we like *and* those we do not like.

To care for someone you do not like requires considerable self regard. So much of what dominates human relationships is competition and trying to be acceptable because we are better than other persons. Rather than lifting ourselves, or feeling self-confident about where we are, we chip away at other persons, hoping to reduce them to a level below us. Only when we have a healthy self-love can we love another.

Love is a feeling, yet more than a feeling. Love really depends upon what we do when we do not feel like it. When Jesus talks about loving our enemies, that surely means something more than liking them. Anger directed at a husband or a wife, a child or a parent, does not mean that love is forever lost. In fact, that anger may be an expression of love.

The feeling of agape love is for the other person, but is something different than an emotional affection. This kind of love is an expression of the Divine.

The presence of God in the expression of love is illustrated in one of Tolstoy's greatest stories, entitled, "Where Love Is, God Is." It is the story of Martin, an old cobbler. Martin is reading about Christ and wishes that Christ would visit him. He falls asleep, and in his sleep, he is startled by a voice which says, "Martin, Martin, look into the street tomorrow; I will come!"

The old cobbler cannot decide. Was the voice real? Or was it just a dream?

The next day he goes continually to the window to look out into the street, "Will he indeed come, I wonder? It is too much to expect, and yet, such things have happened."

During the day, the old man looks out into the street and sees there a cold, shivering sweeper. He brings the sweeper in from the street, gives him tea and invites him to warm his hands by the fire.

Then he invites in a soldier's wife whom he sees from the window trying to wrap her tiny baby in an old, tattered cloth. He gives her food and drink and comfort. Then he brings into his room an apple-woman and the boy who had stolen an apple and run away. He talks to her and her anger disappears. And when they go out again, the boy is helping the woman to carry the load.

The story ends with Martin at a table where a single candle is burning. Martin says to himself, "The day is nearly over and he hasn't been here. It must have been a dream, after all. Yet his voice seemed so real."

As the old cobbler sits there, the figure of the sweeper rises up before his eyes. He hears a voice.

"Martin, Martin, do you not know me? This is I."

Then the figure of the soldier's wife with the child in her arms comes from out of the darkness. Martin hears the voice, "And this is I."

Then comes the figure of the apple-woman and the voice says, "And this, also, is I."

The truth comes to the cobbler that God has come near to him in these persons, that in loving service to men and women and children he has actually met and served the Christ.

There are verses of scripture that give summary to the Tolstoy tale. Those verses are like a nativity:

> In this the love of God was made manifest among us, that God sent his only Son into the world, so that we might live through him (1 John 4:9).

> He who does not love, does not know God; for God is love (1 John 4:8).

Love is not conditional, but love is very demanding. Love is not conditional—that is, love does not demand that you do certain things, or be a certain way, and on condition that you do it, then you can be loved.

Love comes as an expression of grace. When we love other persons, it is not because they "deserve" it, but simply because we are drawn to love. If we loved only when others deserved to be loved, it would become like a business transaction; it would not be love, but coin.

One of Graham Greene's novels is called *Travels With My Aunt.* It is a story of a minor banking official who, in his retirement years, becomes much better acquainted with his "aunt," and even does some travel with her. But she is a rather shady character. And at one point, the man was confronted with the police and their desire to collect information. The question for the man was whether he would try to protect his aunt, or whether he would simply let the police find whatever they could. In thinking and acting this through, Graham Greene gives to the narrating and central character this thought: "Loyalty to a person inevitably entails loyalty to all the imperfections of a human being, even to the chicanery and immorality from which my aunt was not entirely free."

Love comes to the whole person. Love is aware that there are barnacles and warts around, but love loves anyway. Love sees the brokenness and embraces all the parts; the embrace is what enables the other to hold together and live. Love endures, in spite of anything.

Love accepts, but love is also very demanding. We can be very tolerant of our neighbor's child smoking marijuana. We can laugh when it is in someone else's family that a person gets drunk. When we see a person drifting, without seeming involvement in anything, we can be quite patient about that. We can say, "Just give him time." But it is not so easy to say if it is our child. If we really love our children, care what happens, and sense that some of our own life investment and destiny is in them, then we are not tolerant, we do not laugh. We are not patient. It is not easy.

Because we love, we become demanding. We identify with the welfare of the other person and we yearn for him/her to realize the good that is possible in their lives. Love is given whether the demand is met or not, but if you love, you care about what happens to the other person.

Love is expressed in confrontation as well as quiet harmony. By nature, I am one who treasures harmony. When there have been sharp personal differences, I have not felt comfortable either in confronting or in being confronted. My more likely way to cope with the differences has been to avoid or to withdraw from the person with whom I have had the difference. I am speaking now of personal differences. I do not feel that I have withdrawn from controversial issues or avoided uncomfortable tasks. Rather, in personal relations, I have tended not to be a confronter. And when confronted, I have been easily defeated. I have had difficulty in seeing love in those who boldly confront.

In the matter of confronting, I am struggling to learn. The home in which I was raised had continual conflict, and that, I think, contributes to my having treasured too much a tranquility in human affairs. I have needed to learn to "fight."

Differences do exist. These differences may just be matters of personal taste. But they may also be matters of deep moral and spiritual concern. When we are close to others, as in the family or in the church, it is essential in love, to confront rather than withdraw from each other.

A considerable body of literature has developed over the past decade dealing with conflict resolution in marriage. That is our closest human relationship, and it is the first place where we must learn to creatively confront each other. If we can take understanding of creativity from Rollo May, it is precisely in that encounter that the creativity of a marriage can occur. Bach and Wyden in *The Intimate Enemy* seek to document from their work at the Institute of Group Psychotherapy that "verbal conflict between intimates is not only acceptable, especially between husbands and wives; it is constructive and highly desirable."

One of the best resources I have found for "rules" in confrontation is *Love and Negotiate* by John Scanzoni. Its writing is especially directed to conflict in marriage, and thus, deals with the relationship between men and women (confronting the view of dominance and submission) and the implications of conflict for intimacy. I believe the ideas which he presents in the context of marriage are applicable to conflict in the church, which is a larger family.

Scanzoni makes much of the need to confront and negotiate as a matter of justice. Negotiation, he defines as "a process of give and take between two (or more) parties aimed at arriving at a solution or compromise in which each gets something, but not all, that each originally wanted." The author cites many biblical precedents for negotiation, one of them being Micah 6:6-8, "In this sense justice means giving what you should to others, and not taking what you shouldn't. To be just is to be fair, to be *equitable.*" Negotiation is the way to arrive at what is fair. The style of Christian negotiation is mutual submission, as set forth by Paul in Ephesians 5:21, "be subject to one another."

Certain principles of negotiation can be followed that embody love:

1. Bargain in good faith; that is, respond to any serious suggestion or offer made by the other. When one party rejects an offer, he/she is obligated to put forth some kind of counter offer.

2. The objective, when love is present, is maximum joint profit, rather than maximum individual profit.

3. Be aware whether you are negotiating goals or means. If you are agreed on goals, the negotiating is much simpler.

4. Develop the capability of switching bargaining strategies. Concentrate on the objective, ignoring such diversionary tactics as name calling.

5. Avoid getting into deadlocks over issues that matter a great deal to you, especially where time is a crucial factor in the decision, by keeping an equality of power and by maintaining a willingness to negotiate.

6. Be a reconciler. Genuine smiles and a gentle, loving demeanor are always important. Convey a commitment of love even in the midst of the battle. Love is not interested in winning and losing, but in negotiating an acceptable understanding.

7. Be dependable to observe negotiated agreements.

8. Be sensitive to critical points in negotiation at which to resolve or de-escalate; otherwise, sharper conflict will ensue.

Scanzoni also identifies several strategies in negotiation, among them, anger. He speaks of the positive value of anger in that it can communicate a level of feeling. There are also risks in anger, depending upon the course it takes. A loving relationship seeks to avoid physical or psychic violence in anger.

There was a time when we were impressed when a spouse would tell of the love he or she has known in marriage by declaring, "My husband and I have never had a cross word," or "My wife and I have never had an argument." Such words are now seen as describing an unfortunate relationship that involves complete submission on the part of one, and the failure of two personalities to both emerge fully. Such a description now sounds deadly to us. To love is to encounter the other—in marriage and in all human relationships.

CONCERNING THE CORINTHIAN TEXT

There is no finer description of love in scripture or in all of literature than this chapter. It is one of the most familiar of passages, one of the most frequently read. Common it is to the wedding ceremony. Our very familiarity with it may obscure its meaning. Read it anew and slowly absorb its meaning.

Love is the greatest of all things. Speech without love is noise. Knowledge, even religious knowledge, is nothing without love. Even if I do all things good, sacrifice my life, but do not act in love, I will not find it satisfying.

Paul does not give us a definition of love. Rather, he describes how love works. He uses both positive and negative terms. In the positive terms, love is patient and kind. It has enduring quality in what it encounters, what it believes, and what it hopes. In negative terms, love is not jealous, boastful, arrogant, rude, selfish, irritable, resentful. Love is not happy when misfortune falls to the other person. Love is able to enter into the joy of another person.

Love is not only the greatest, it endures. It has permanence. Paul also speaks of love as maturity. He would give up the childish, which is the absence of love. Being childish is to be distinguished from childlikeness. It is to be remembered that Jesus said that whoever did not become as a child would not enter the kingdom. His saying is to be understood as referring to certain qualities of children, especially those which express openness and eagerness. But to be childish is not a part of the kingdom. To love is to give up childish ways.

Of all the things which endure, love is the greatest.

CONCERNING CREATIVITY

A rather tragic self-assessment occurs frequently when persons declare, "I am not creative." All persons can be creative. That does not mean that we are all artists or poets, activities around which people often associate exclusively with creativity.

Rollo May defines creativity as the process of bringing something new into being. That process is centered in an encounter, a confrontation, and May illustrates the encounter drawing from the experience of art. Note, in the illustration, the encounter is not something that involves the artist alone. The artist may be alone in the encounter. But after the encounter, that which emerges has a corporate impact. Something new has come into being and that affects others.

Significant for us is to relate this creativity to the human encounter.

FOR FURTHER CONSIDERATION

• Think of the contribution to life of all the forms of love found in the four Greek terms.

• How can you act on behalf of a person who is antagonistic toward you?

• Do you see a difference between liking and loving? Were there persons Jesus did not like?

• Have you been unable, at some time, to receive the love that has been offered? Have you offered love that was not received?

• Can you identify examples when religious knowledge has not been shared in love?

• What is the difference between being "irritable" and being angry?

• Are there persons in the congregation that you avoid? What might happen if you encountered them?

SOME ACTIVITIES

Plan a study in conflict resolution, using a text such as *The Love-Fight* by David W. Augsburger.

Demonstrate and practice such communication skills as "the shared meaning" and "active listening."

Use "strength bombardment," taking turns in telling each person in the group what you appreciate about them.

Write a letter to someone who seems distant to you.

Engage in some physical labor that is not your responsibility, but that will express love.

Read A Litany of "Rites and Ordinances" as a class.

A Litany of "Rites and Ordinances"

God is a deity who is all powerful, whose promises are great, including life eternal and all the gifts of grace. Likewise, great is the punishment of those who deny the Gospel. Therefore, we are moved out of love to call attention to the things which Christ commanded.

Tell us, where in Holy Scripture is outward water baptism found?

As early as Noah's time, God began to reveal a prefiguration of the water baptism of the New Covenant. Such a revelation is found, also, in the time of Moses as the seed of Abraham escaped through the sea. Finally, when God wished to reveal his Son to the world, he sent a forerunner, John the Baptizer, who would baptize Jesus.

Was Jesus baptized merely as an example to us?

It was God's plan for him, "For thus it is fitting for us to fulfill all righteousness." Beyond his own baptism, Jesus wished to found and ordain a water bath for his entire church, that it should be a seal and symbol of all who believe in Him.

Concerning the Lord's Supper, how was it instituted by Christ?

True believers were commanded to proclaim his death on the cross, break the bread of Communion, and covenant with one another in love as members of Christ.

Are we to take responsibility for the sin of other members of the body? Can we remain in fellowship with one who is evil?

There is a necessary separation in the New Covenant between believers and nonbelievers. The member cannot truly be of the body of the Lord unless cleansed by true penitence and repentance.

What if dissension arises in the church?

Let the member who creates dissension walk in simplicity, in obedience of faith, in peace and in unity, submitting to the other members, after the counsel of Peter.

Is it possible to prove our faith by appealing to Scripture?

To appeal to Scripture and to believe in Scripture are two vastly different things. The believer outwardly reads the Scripture in faith and inwardly hears the word of life that gives strength and power to follow Jesus.

What are the rewards for the one who denies self and follows Christ, enduring the cross and suffering to the very end?

Blessings and glories of such great dignity and joy and love will be obtained through Christ that no human tongue can express it, nor can be described what is prepared for those who love God. We will together praise and glorify our God forever. Amen.

Adapted from the writing of Alexander Mack

RESOURCES FOR ADDITIONAL STUDY
Augsburger, David W. *Cherishable: Love and Marriage.* Scottdale, Pa.: Herald Press, 1971.

_____. *The Love-Fight*. Scottdale, Pa.: Herald Press, 1973.

Christ, Carol P. and Plaskow, Judith. *Womanspirit Rising*. New York: Harper-Row, 1979.

Kennedy, Eugene. *A Time for Being Human*. St. Louis: Cornerstone, 1978.

May, Rollo. *Love and Will*. New York: Dell, 1974.

Mayeroff, Milton. *On Caring*. New York: Harper-Row, 1971.

Padovano, Anthony. *Free to Be Faithful*. Ramsey, N.J.: Paulist.

Phelps, Stanlee and Austin, Nancy. *The Assertive Woman*. San Luis Obispo: Impact Press, 1975.

Powell, John. *Unconditional Love*. Niles, Ill.: Argus Comm., 1978.

_____. *Why Am I Afraid to Tell You Who I Am?* Niles, Ill.: Argus Comm., 1969.

Scanzoni, John. *Love and Negotiate*. Waco, Texas: Word, 1979.

To love tenderly
by claiming God's gift of recon-
ciliation in the family, the
church, society, and among all
nations and all faiths.

8   TOWARD
RECONCILIATION

Peace on earth and mercy mild,
God and sinners reconciled!
CHARLES WESLEY

Therefore, if any one is in Christ, he is a new creation; and the old has passed away, behold, the new has come. All this is from God, who through Christ reconciled us to himself and gave us the ministry of reconciliation; that is, God was in Christ reconciling the world to himself, not counting their trespasses against them, and entrusting to us the message of reconciliation. So we are ambassadors for Christ, God making his appeal through us. We beseech you on behalf of Christ, be reconciled to God.

2 Corinthians 5:17-20

Therefore remember that at one time you Gentiles in the flesh, called the uncircumcision by what is called the circumcision, which is made in the flesh by hands — remember that you were at that time separated from Christ, alienated from the commonwealth of Israel, and strangers to the covenants of promise, having no hope and without God in the world. But now in Christ Jesus you who once were far off have been brought near in the blood of Christ. For he is our peace, who has made us both one, and has broken down the dividing wall of hostility, by abolishing in his flesh the law of commandments and ordinances, that he might create in himself one new man in place of the two, so making peace, and might reconcile us both to God in one body through the cross, thereby bringing the hostility to an end. And he came and preached peace to you who were far off and peace to those who were near; for through him we both have access in one Spirit to the Father. So then you are no longer strangers and sojourners, but you are fellow citizens with the saints and members of the household of God, built upon the foundation of the apostles and prophets, Christ Jesus himself being the cornerstone, in whom the whole structure is joined together and grows into a holy temple in the Lord; in whom you also are built into it for a dwelling place of God in the Spirit.

Ephesians 2:11-22

Conversion means being turned round so as to be by faith and in foretaste a participant in and an agent of God's reign. The proper question is not: Are there few that be saved? The question is: Who is doing the will of God? To speak of the finality of Christ is not, primarily, to speak of the fate of those who do not accept him as Lord; discussion often proceeds as if it were. It is to say that commitment to Christ in the fellowship of those who share the same commitment is the clue to a true participation in God's purpose for his whole creation. The privileges to which conversion is the gateway are not exclusive claims upon God's grace; they are the privileges of those who have been chosen for special responsibility in the carrying out of God's blessed design. Their joy will be not that they are saved, but that God's name is hallowed, his will done and his reign perfected. There are many hints in the Bible which suggest that this saving purpose will extend beyond those who are its conscious agents. Indeed the metaphor of salt, used of the disciples, suggests that the Church has a function to the world which extends far beyond the boundaries of its own membership.

Lesslie Newbigin,
The Finality of Christ

RECONCILIATION RANKS high in the hierarchy of Brethren emphases and values. Concern for reconciliation among the Brethren comes as early as Alexander Mack for whom Matthew 18 was familiar territory, and it is as recent as the latest baptism, for in baptizing, our church has often pointed to the Matthew passage as a way of identifying how the Christian is to live in community after the immersion:

If your brother sins against you, go and tell him his fault, between you and him alone. If he listens to you, you have gained your brother. But if he does not listen, take one or two others along with you, that every word may be confirmed by the evidence of two or three witnesses. If he refuses to listen to them, tell it to the church; and if he refuses to listen even to the church, let him be to you as a Gentile and a tax collector (Matthew 18:15-17).

Then Peter came up and said to him, "Lord, how often shall my brother sin against me, and I forgive him? As many as seven times?" Jesus said to him, "I do not say to you seven times, but seventy times seven" (Matthew 18:21, 22).

Reconciliation refers to a coming together of one's spirit with God's Spirit, as a reuniting, and in everyday life, reflecting that togetherness. Reconciliation is to make consistent or compatible; for the Christian, it is being consistent with God's intention for life. For the Christian, reconciliation is being compatible, not opposed, to the rest of God's creation. Reconciliation is to restore in relationship, as when a person feels forsaken by God or alienated from God, as when nations struggle with each other in enmity; as when different faith perspectives and loyalties are suspicious and hostile to each other; as when two people battle in estrangement.

Reconciliation rekindles the love in a couple who would have divorced. Reconciliation draws back into active fellowship, the church member who withdrew because she was unhappy with the way the church budget was being spent. Reconciliation brings to a common table all of the ethnic factions when they break bread with each other. Reconciliation is a foreign policy that forgets old enmities and lives in mutual trust. Reconciliation recognizes differences in belief but discovers a common search.

Dale Brown, a professor at Bethany Theological Seminary, offers an understanding of reconciliation that issues from the Matthew 18 text:

> Perhaps we need to learn anew the biblical truth that genuine reconciliation comes through confrontation. There is no easy reconciliation apart from judgment and the agony of the cross. It may be possible to derive such a confrontive and reconciling style from new applications of Matthew 18:15-20, a passage which, read before Brethren baptism, has been instructive to our styles of settling differences. We have been taught that the first step in reconciliation is to confront our brother with that which we have against him.

There is a sense in which our reconciliation with God comes with such confrontation. That is, the Spirit confronts us and convinces us of a new way. This is the experience of conversion. We are not reconciled with God without first becoming aware of how our lives are contrary to God's intention. Reconciliation comes, not because we have fully attained God's purpose, but as a gift.

In realizing reconciliation with those around us, we typically look for ways of reconciling that will be easy. We do not expect it to demand the energy of confrontation. Despite the frequent use of Matthew 18 by the Brethren, there are many who feel that the Brethren have a special problem in being confrontive. Those who make this observation say that it is because of our peace teaching; that we have so internalized the necessity to live at peace that we deny points of conflict, and when we do engage in confrontation or conflict, we feel guilty about it. To deny that we are offended, or to carry with us the burden of guilt because we have confronted, certainly does not make us receptive to reconciliation. Indeed, the alienation grows.

In the reconciliation process, *it is always the responsibility of the one who is offended,* who feels that he or she has been wronged, *to take the first step.* If you are hurt because of what a relative has said about you, it is first your responsibility, not that of the relative, to restore the fellowship. If your employer has acted unjustly toward you, it is your responsibility to yourself and to the employer, to confront that injustice and to seek justice. In whatever circumstance we are wherein we have grievance, it rests, first of all, with us to initiate action. This is not only the pattern suggested in Matthew 18, but holds practical wisdom. The one who has offended may feel no need for a change, or may not even be aware of the offense. And, in many instances, when the offended takes the initiative to confront a person with a specific issue, an entirely new understanding comes. The offender has an opportunity to explain. Or, the offender has the opportunity to correct.

Following Matthew 18 does not always bring reconciliation. There is that shadow side to our lives that realizes less than we are promised. Even Jesus recognized that, "let him be to you as a Gentile and a tax collector" (Matthew 18:17). It is likewise instructive to read the final verse of the eleventh chapter of Hebrews. In that chapter we have a roll call of the faithful, bringing together such disparate persons as Moses and Rahab the harlot, Sarah and Samson, and several more. "And all these, though well attested by faith, did not receive what was promised . . . "

The promised reconciliation does not always come. One of the greatest tragedies of life, I feel, is when there is a total estrangement between parent and child. I know parents who have a daughter who has broken off contact with them. Every effort they make as an act of friendship and love is rebuffed. The daughter does not say why she has removed herself. She offers no basis for negotiation. She just wants nothing to do with the parents. I know other parents who have a son who never responds to a gift they give nor takes any initiative to contact them. He is not hostile to them, but just "tuned out." He speaks vaguely of things that happened years ago in his childhood that bother him. I know a child whose parents have "disowned" her because she has done something that they disapprove. They no longer call her their daughter. They do not want to see her or acknowledge her.

What is a Christian to do when efforts at reconciliation are rebuffed? And, while the one who is offended has the responsibility to confront, suppose that member of the family, or that member of the church, does not, but withdraws. What then? So far as we can, we are to live as if the gift of reconciliation had been received.

The need for reconciliation is beyond the personal. We are accustomed to thinking only of our personal involvement. An illustration of how corporate we are came vividly to me in 1966. I had landed in Lagos, Nigeria, on January 15, on the first flight into the airport after the bloody coup which left dead a respected prime minister and several other state officials. The next day, I was walking on the streets of Lagos when I fell into conversation with a young Nigerian. He had mistaken me for an European, and when he discovered that I was American, his attitude changed abruptly. Later that evening, I wrote notes of the exchange which followed.

"You had better go immediately to the airport and return to your country."

"Why?" I asked, and told him I wanted to stay a bit longer to learn to know him and his people. He did not want that, and it would be better for me if I left now.

"Do you know what happened in the Congo?" he inquired. "It could happen here. Then, when your skin is not black, you are in danger."

Then he turned on me accusingly, "How are the black people treated in the United States? Do you treat them right?"

They were not always treated right, I had to admit.

"Why?" he demanded.

My answers were poor and they came haltingly. I was uncomfortable, and he knew it. "Because some people do not understand," I said.

"Do not understand what?"

"That black and white are equal."

"What are you doing to make them equal?"

"We are passing laws for better education, better housing, voting."

"When will they be equal, black and white?"

"It will take time," I told him.

"Why does it take time?" Then with fury he nearly shouted, "Why do you turn dogs on my people?" Had he been in possession of dogs at the moment, I have no doubt he would have gotten even with me.

This exchange came nearly fifteen years ago when our nation was in the midst of the civil rights revolution. Pictures were going over the world of dogs being turned on demonstrators. And in such foreign places, when we go to them, we are not simply an individual. We are a corporate person, embodying our own nation, race, religion, history, and sex. As that corporate person, we can become quickly aware of the need for reconciliation in the world. Then we know that we have been given the ministry of reconciliation.

We look to persons and to institutions to embody and to symbolize our ministries. We understand Christian service better because of a program known as Brethren Volunteer Service and Sister Theresa. We can visualize peacemaking through persons like Ora Huston and institutions such as the Glen Cree Reconciliation Centre in the Republic of Ireland. We know the simple life more fully when we see it lived in a community like Reba Place or find persons in our own congregation whose simple living is to them a joy. We are more aware of possibilities in commitment when we study the Church of the Savior. In a similar way, we look for reconciliation in the world and our lives are called to be parables of reconciliation.

One illustration of corporate reconciliation being expressed to the world is found in Hiroshima, Japan. There in a city that is the world's most visible symbol of the ultimate meaning of nuclear warfare, Barbara Reynolds, a Quaker, began in 1965, the World Friendship Center. The Center is a hostel, hosting international and national guests with

lodging, meals and information. The Center provides services to persons who were victims of the 1945 atomic bombing. It is a cultural center. It is a peace center, seeking to be active in various peace efforts.

The World Friendship Center offers a religious presence to the city. The President of the Center from the time of its beginning has been Dr. Tomin Harada, a surgeon who is a Buddhist. Most of the members of the Riji Kai (Board of Directors) are devotees of the Buddhist and/or Shinto faith. Working at the Center, helping to direct the work have been Brethren, Mennonites and Quakers from the United States. Brethren who have served there include Ira and Mabel Moomaw and Leona Row Eller.

There is an American Committee who has helped to support the Center, including the provision of personnel and the engaging in exchange programs. The Committee has received support from the Disciples of Christ and the Unitarian Universalists, as well as the historic peace churches.

The presence of Christians in the Center is a witness. Although the Center is not a Christian institution, one of its activities has been Bible study.

How is the World Friendship Center a symbol of reconciliation? It represents an effort to be friends to persons of all nations. There have been efforts to push the Riji Kai to a more extreme position in its peace work—a position which would shut off relationships with South Africa and which would have condemned the United States during the Vietnam War. While the Center has been clear in its opposition to the war in Vietnam and to apartheid, the Riji Kai has avoided a strongly political stance or aligning itself with more extreme groups in order that it might achieve its goal of being a center of friendship to all the nations of the world.

The Center reflects a reconciliation between former enemies. The American personnel in Hiroshima are important, more important for this form of reconciliation than for citizens of any other nation because of American responsibility for the bombing. Here are peoples of nations, formerly enemies and even now vulnerable to enmity arising from economic competition, who now live and work together as friends. And now they have a new enemy: warfare and especially nuclear warfare.

The Center embodies a form of reconciliation among religious faiths. Those who are Christian have joined with those of other faiths in prayers and meditations. There has been the opportunity to explore the religions that are represented there.

There is a sense in which reconciliation among the faiths is the most difficult form of reconciliation. Religion goes to the ultimate meaning of life. It is the search for and the affirming of Truth. And it may seem to be that part of life which has the least room for reconciliation because other religions are understood as heresies and for

Christians, relations with other faiths may seem a violation of the Divine command against playing "the harlot after their gods" (Exodus 34:15).

The biblical writers had a vision of the oneness of the human family. The parable of the Last Judgment (Matthew 25:31-46) speaks of the Son of Man in glory, "Before him will be gathered all the nations . . . " And Jesus, in his high priestly prayer for the Church prayed for unity, "that they may all be one" (John 17:20). Yet we have difficulty realizing that unity within Christianity, much less with all nations and all faiths. Indeed, within the denomination, we sometimes need reconciliation. And in a single congregation.

Many Christians have assumed that Christianity would continue to grow and that other religions would simply disappear as soon as the message gets to everyone. Periodically, there are grandiose schemes to "win the world to Christ in one generation." That form of being triumphant by Christianity seems unlikely. There is a dynamic spirit in other world faiths that will not fold and go away. Our ministry of reconciliation will be in a world where there are not only diverse understandings of Christianity, but other vital world faiths as well.

How am I to be reconciled to this condition? First, God has not called me to make a judgment about the eternal destiny of those who are not Christian as I am. It would be hell for me to be outside of Christ, but I cannot move from that statement to say that all non-Christians are condemned by God to hell. I can be reconciling by being content to let God be our judge.

Second, I can learn from other faiths. That does not mean that I believe I will learn something beyond my Christianity. I believe in the wholeness and completeness of Christianity. By the witness of another faith, I may discover something in my own that I had not seen before.

Third, I can discover with those of other faiths a common spirit—a spirit that is at one in its affirmation of the Holy and of Creation, and standing over against irreligion and secularism. In the other religions of the world, Christians can find allies in the struggle for peace and justice.

And, fourth, I find reconciliation, not by being a lukewarm Christian, not by trying to remove all the offenses of the Gospel, but by affirming strongly and concretely my faith. It is precisely when I am most Christian that I have the greatest opportunity for reconciliation with those of other faiths. Again, I find in this fact an echo of Matthew 18.

CONCERNING THE CORINTHIAN TEXT

Paul writes to the Corinthian Church about the miracle of new life, being in Christ, a new creation. Think of how radical that statement is. The one in Christ is not a retread, not reformed, not, like our commercial products, "new and improved." A new creation! He even gives it a time perspective. The old has passed away. The new has come.

The new creation is the gift of God. It is the work of redemption which Christ has done. In Christ, we are reconciled or brought again into relationship with God. Once reconciled, we are given or charged with the ministry of reconciliation.

Paul explains what he means by the ministry of reconciliation. That ministry declares the reconciling and forgiving work of Jesus Christ. Once we are the new creation, we become ambassadors representing this reconciled state; God's appeal is made through us.

CONCERNING THE EPHESIAN TEXT

The lesson from Ephesians pictures the unity which God intends. Those who are far off are brought near. Paul shows especially the reconciliation of Jew and Gentile. Hostilities are brought to an end. Christ is our peace. The lower status of those "outsiders" is no more; we are all now fellow-citizens and saints in the household of God.

CONCERNING THE FINALITY OF CHRIST

What is the place of Christ in the meaning and direction of history? Lesslie Newbigin, in a little volume called *The Finality of Christ,* explores such a question. He has done so from the perspective of a missionary in India where he was in direct and open relationship with other faiths. This brief excerpt can provide some insight to us as a people who are increasingly in contact with other churches, other cults, other faiths.

FOR FURTHER CONSIDERATION

• Can you recall times when you deliberately followed the counsel of Matthew 18:15-20?

• Why do we experience disunity in the Body of Christ?

• How does being reconciled with God aid in reconciliation within the human family?

• Consider times when as individuals we become corporate beings, needing reconciliation with those who see us as representing something to which we belong.

• Do you see ways in which you and your congregation could be actively involved with those of another faith?

SOME ACTIVITIES

Review the ministries of reconciliation of your congregation and of the whole Church of the Brethren.

Plan an evening of faith dialogue with adherents of another religion.

Study the relationship of Christianity with Judaism and Islam.

Share information about the World and National and your own local Council of Churches as one form of unity within the Christian Church.

RESOURCES FOR ADDITIONAL STUDY

Brown, Dale. *Brethren and Pacifism*. Elgin: Brethren Press, 1970.

Burtt, Edwin A. *Man Seeks the Divine*. New York: Harper-Row, 1970.

Fellows, Ward. *Religions East and West*. New York: Holt, Rinehart, and Winston, Inc., 1979.

Hopfe, Lewis. *Religions of the World*. Riverside, N.J.: Glencoe, 1976.

Newbigin, Lesslie. *The Finality of Christ*. Atlanta: John Knox, 1969.

Smith, Huston. *The Religions of Man*. New York: Harper-Row, 1965.

Swartz, Fred W. *All in God's Family*. Elgin: Brethren Press, 1977.

To walk humbly
    by diligently searching the
scriptures.

9

THE
DILIGENT
SEARCH

*The words of the Gospel are
not sweetness and light, but
salt and light.*
WILLIAM BEAHM

Thy word is a lamp to my feet
and a light to my path.
I have sworn an oath and confirmed it,
to observe thy righteous ordinances.
I am sorely afflicted;
give me life, O Lord, according to thy word!
Accept my offerings of praise, O Lord,
and teach me thy ordinances.
I hold my life in my hand continually,
but I do not forget thy law.
The wicked have laid a snare for me,
but I do not stray from thy precepts.
Thy testimonies are my heritage for ever;
yea, they are the joy of my heart.
I incline my heart to perform thy statutes
for ever, to the end.

Psalm 119:105-112

All scripture is inspired by God and profitable for teaching, for reproof, for correction, and for training in righteousness, that the man of God may be complete, equipped for every good work.

2 Timothy 3:16, 17

We affirm that the Bible, rightly interpreted, is a fully trustworthy guide for our lives. In this sense we reaffirm our historic understanding of scripture as an infallible rule of faith and practice. With these and other expressions we honor and acknowledge the unique authority of the Bible for the church.

We affirm the need to interpret scripture in the light of scripture. When we fail to discern how a particular text relates to the rest of the Bible, we are likely to distort its meaning or press its significance in an unbiblical way. We agree that we need to weigh scripture against scripture rather than appeal to favorite texts while ignoring others.

We affirm that all scripture must be interpreted in the light of God's self-revelation in Jesus Christ. While God speaks to us through all parts of the Bible, we must read the Old Testament in the light of the New, and the New in terms of its witness to God's gift of life in Jesus Christ. It is Jesus Christ who is truly the Word of God made flesh and through whom we perceive scripture as one unified account of redemption.

We affirm the need for a careful, disciplined approach to the study of the Bible. This calls for the use of the best texts and translations available to us. It also calls for sensitivity to the literary and historical context of passages we wish to study. Undergirding all such study must be an openness to the same Spirit who inspired the biblical message.

We affirm the central importance of the gathered community of believers in the interpretation of the Bible. Together with our forebears, we are convinced that all individual insights into scripture need to be tested in and by the community. When it is functioning properly, the church will be a place where the gifts and insights of all will contribute to a more complete understanding of God's word.

We affirm that a faithful response to the biblical message involves both believing and doing. It is the doers of the word who will be justified in God's sight, and not those who give only lip service to its claims. At the same time, obedience with our lives does not come about apart from a joyful, trusting acceptance of the biblical message and its authority for our lives.

1979 Church of the Brethren Annual Conference
Biblical Inspiration and Authority

HUMAN LIFE seems to depend upon authority. We could not live as a society without authority vested in some governing body and in institutions. We respond to authority in diverse ways. Some like things to be done in an authoritarian way, whether by government, or by school, or by church. At the other extreme, some are quite anti-authority, and react negatively to any authority that is imposed from the outside. Regardless of our attitude toward authority, we all look to authority, even if we make ourselves the authority. In matters of belief, heresy is precisely that, making oneself the authority. The word *heresy* comes from the Greek term *hairesis*, which means *the act of choosing*. Heresy is choosing oneself as the authority.

The Christian recognizes four sources of authority in our faith: Scripture, the Church, the fellowship, and the inner light.

Scripture. So central is the Bible to the followers of Jesus Christ that we have often been called "a people of the Book." The Annual Conference of 1979 recorded understandings within the Church of the Brethren that help to make clear why scripture is of central importance to us as authority. The Conference declared: "Both the biblical writers and those whose witness contributed to their message were empowered and guided by the Holy Spirit. Because of this presence of God enabling and equipping the biblical writers, we hear God's own word addressing us through the words of scripture."

The Bible is a witness to God's activity during one period of time and God's promises for the time in which we live and in the time to come. Therefore, there is authority concerning what God is like and what God intends and is likely to do. The Bible records the covenant between God and the people of God, and, thus, becomes an authority for the nature and content of our relationship when we live as a covenant people. The Bible is the sole source of the information we have about Jesus of Nazareth and the context in which he became the Christ. Therefore, the Bible must be our first authority in knowing the life and death and teachings of Jesus.

The Bible contains many types of writing, including faith-myth, history, poetry, wisdom, oracles, letters, teachings. In our study of scripture, we are to have three centers of foci: 1) *Events* such as Creation, Exodus, Settlement, Exile, Crucifixion and Resurrection; 2) *Persons*, THE PERSON, Jesus Christ, and other great personalities from whom we learn, such as Abraham and Sarah, Moses, David, Isaiah and Jeremiah, Mary, Peter and Paul; 3) *Great ideas* such as grace, forgiveness, redemption, reconciliation and resurrection.

The Bible is a faith document. It was written by those who were in a faith relationship with God. It was recognized as canon by those who were being faithful.

Its truth opens to the faithful, especially the seekers. Those who come to scripture to battle it, to discredit it, will have their little victory. Those who come to scripture to understand, to be inspired, will also know victory. Come then to scripture with expectancy, with reverence, with a wholeness of heart and mind, and a commitment to the One who is revealed there.

In such an attitude, the Brethren have approached the scripture, "interpreting the Old Testament in light of the New Testament." That is, the Brethren have affirmed the fulness of revelation in Jesus Christ; therefore, if there is material in the Old Testament that is not consistent with the New, we are guided by the New. (It is also correct to say that we interpret the New Testament in light of the Old, in that the Old Testament provides the context and the preparation for the New.) Within the New Testament, we have given priority to the teachings of Jesus. In instances where there is conflicting evidence or an absence of material in the New Testament, we have sought "the mind of Christ" based upon the totality of his person and teachings.

The Church. In times past, Protestants tended to emphasize scripture as authority while Roman Catholics tended to emphasize the Church. The reformers pointed to scripture in contrast to papal or council statements. Roman Catholics, on the other hand, tended to look, in the first instance, to the Church for authority. Catholics have pointed toward the fact that the scripture comes from the Church and that through the centuries the Church has been the preserver, interpreter, and teacher of the Bible. As some Catholics have said, "For authority, we do not go first to the Bible. We go to the Mother Church with the Bible in her hands."

There is today less distance between Protestants and Catholics on the matter of authority. They are increasingly looking to scripture and are encouraging laity to study the Bible in ways that are new. Most Protestant groups are taking more seriously the wisdom and truth that is embodied in the Church.

Historically, the Church of the Brethren paid scant attention to the great creeds of the Church, being anti-creedal or at least, non-creedal. The early Brethren ignored the Early Church Fathers and were at least as critical as appreciative of the Reformers. However, there did develop a profound respect for the Annual Meeting. The Annual Meeting was and is the final authority in the governing of the Church. Members also looked to the Annual Meeting for direction in such matters as belief and behavior and dress.

The authority of the Church includes the writings that have come to us through the history of the Church, as the Church has spoken through assembled councils and as the Church has spoken through its prophets, such as St. Augustine, St. Francis of Assisi, Martin Luther, John Calvin, Walter Rauschenbusch, Karl Barth, Rosemary Ruether, and Harvey Cox. Within our own tradition, we look with particular interest to the thinking of Alexander Mack, our founder, to such a writing as William Beahm's *Studies in Christian Belief,* and to the corporate statements of the Church such as the "Annual Conference Statement on Tithing and Christian Stewardship." To give these sources authority means to want to know what is being said, to take them seriously, and to let them make a difference in your own judgments.

The Fellowship. A third source of authority is the fellowship. It is a part of the Church, but in this instance, it is that body of believers known to you personally and intimately. It is those with whom you interact directly. It is an expression of the faith community.

We grant to the fellowship authority, believing that the Holy Spirit can speak through such a gathering. The person who is struggling with a question of faith or is considering a course of action can find counsel that is enormously helpful. Or that counsel may be offered through a pastor or a friend.

The importance of this form of authority is that it represents a dynamic interaction. The likelihood of discovering God's way is much greater than when each simply goes his or her own way.

The Inner Light. The Christian responds to the leading of the Spirit within. Indeed, even in becoming a follower of Christ, the person acknowledges the presence of God in Christ and becomes convinced that God's Spirit is leading. This is the inner light felt by Isaiah in the temple, "Woe is me! For I am lost; for I am a man of unclean lips, and I dwell in the midst of a people of unclean lips; for my eyes have seen the King, the Lord of hosts!" (Isaiah 6:5). It is the inner light seen by Saul of Tarsus," . . . rise and enter the city, and you will be told what you are to do." (Acts 9:6) It is the inner light which came to the apostles when they said, "We must obey God rather than men" (Acts 5:29).

The Brethren have emphasized this inner light, especially in the form of conscience and conscientious objection to war.

Anthony Padovano, a Roman Catholic thinker, speaks of the tension that can develop between the "inner light" of the person and the "outer light" of the church in *Free to Be Faithful.*

> It can happen that a position which is beginning to be seen as doctrinally unsound may not have reached a point where the official Church is able to change it without causing a pastoral tragedy. A few more years may be required before the community of faith is able to appreciate the "wrongness" of a previous position and the suitability of reformulation. During the interim, a believer may be in advance of the official Church, having achieved within himself both doctrinal and pastoral consistency. Such a believer may be called upon to serve as prophet, perhaps to suffer for his prophecy.

This source of authority is unique in that it comes inwardly, while the other three sources are from the outside. Actually, the other three sources, if we give them authority in the right way, also become inner sources—we absorb them, they become a part of us. They do not remain outside as coercive and oppressive. They are authority because we choose them as authority, even when the implications might be uncomfortable for a period of time.

All four sources of authority are needed by the Christian. Strange aberrations from Christianity happen when persons are less than all four, especially, when only one source of authority is recognized. The sources are interrelated, as when the fellowship studies the scriptures, or when the individual conscience is shared with the fellowship. When the sources of authority are not in agreement, then the person must ultimately decide, and when the individual's "inner light" is counter to the other three sources of authority, the individual should proceed to work out his own salvation only with great "fear and trembling." This is not a "do it yourself" system, but is an awareness that God can speak uniquely to a single person.

CONCERNING THE PSALTER TEXT

In the poetry of the Psalmist is forceful affirmation of scripture as authority in life. The word "is a lamp unto my feet, and a light unto my path." The metaphor of light is used, also, by John's Gospel to describe the word. "The true light that enlightens every man (and woman) was coming into the world" (John 1:9). The believer declares obedience to the laws found in the Word; those laws are not forgotten. To hear the scripture is not drudgery, but is a joy to the heart, and the heart is tipped toward the counsel of the scripture.

Read again the passage (vss. 105-112) from the 119th Psalm. If you are in a class situation, the verses could be read in unison as an affirmation.

CONCERNING THE TIMOTHY TEXT

From 2 Timothy comes an endorsement of *all* or every scripture as inspired by God. The writer has reference to what we call the Old Testament. It is reasonable for the Christian to apply this understanding to both Testaments. There are specific understandings to take from 2 Timothy. One is that *all* scripture has value, all is profitable. Therefore, it is a mistake to avoid or to sanitize scripture, to make it fit your own bias. Even when you feel a direct conflict with what is declared in scripture, it is important to continue to study—the scripture speaks to you most forcefully from beyond your present understanding. I recall hearing Markus Barth speak with harsh criticism of church school curriculum and teachers that reshape and tidy biblical stories to "protect" children. Better it is, he said, to let David be David; "tell the story and get out of the way."

A second understanding is that scripture has different uses: teaching, reproof, correction, training in righteousness. Can you identify specific scriptures that would be profitable in each of these four categories?

CONCERNING AFFIRMATIONS FOR BRETHREN TODAY

The quotation from the 1979 Annual Conference given at the beginning of this chapter, lists some of the affirmations made about scripture. Do you make these affirmations? In the full statement, the Conference identified related areas wherein the Brethren are not yet agreed. Secure a copy of the full statement on "Biblical Inspiration and Authority" and study its background and historical material, discuss the affirmations and the disagreements. Do you find the same kind of agreement—disagreement in your congregation? Consider especially the section which speaks about holding "one another in love and fellowship when there exists a diversity of attitudes."

FOR FURTHER CONSIDERATION

• What implications do you see in the fact that the Annual Conference statement illustrates TO WALK HUMBLY with "by diligently searching the scriptures"? Relate humility and the way in which scripture is used.

- Cite examples of weighing scripture against scripture.
- We are all "literalists." That is all of us take literally portions of the Bible. But we all choose what part will be taken literally.
- How do you respond to the following statement: Scripture enters a person more thoroughly by letting it marinate, than by being hit with it as a club.
- Can you identify areas of your life in which you search the scriptures for correction or for training in righteousness?

SOME ACTIVITIES

Plan for exercises in Bible familiarity. For example, select teams and compete in the finding of scripture passages through the use of concordances. Examine together certain passages in a commentary such as the twelve-volume *The Interpreter's Bible*. A class will benefit greatly by knowing and using these basic tools of the concordance and commentaries.

Commit to memory the names in order of the books of the Bible.

Arrange for an adult to offer Bible instruction to the sixth graders in your congregation on a one-to-one basis.

Pray individually or corporately the following prayers. The first is from an unknown source; the second is from *The Book of Common Prayer*.

> Let not thy Word, O Lord,
>   become a judgment upon us,
> that we hear it and do it not,
> that we know it and love it not,
> that we believe it and obey it not.
> O hear and deliver us, we beseech Thee,
>   through Jesus Christ our Lord. Amen.

Blessed Lord, who has caused all holy scriptures to be written for our learning; grant that we may in such wise hear them, read, mark, learn, and inwardly digest them, that by patience, and comfort of thy holy Word, we may embrace, and ever hold fast the blessed hope of everlasting life, which thou hast given us in our Saviour Jesus Christ. Amen.

RESOURCES FOR ADDITIONAL STUDY

Anderson, Bernhard W. *Understanding the Old Testament*. Englewood Cliffs, N.J.: Prentice-Hall, 1975.

Bainton, Roland. *Here I Stand: A Life of Martin Luther*. Nashville: Abingdon, 1978.

Breidenstine, A. G. The Quester Series. Elgin: Brethren Press.

Cadbury, Henry: *Jesus: What Manner of Man?* Naperville, Ill.: Allenson, 1962.

Davies, W. D. *Invitation to the New Testament.* Garden City, N. Y.: Doubleday, 1969.

Gloege, Gerhard. *The Day of His Coming.* Philadelphia: Fortress, 1963.

Gottwald, Norman K. *A Light to the Nations.* New York: Harper-Row, 1959.

Snyder, Graydon F. and Shaffer, Kenneth M., Jr. *Texts in Transit.* Elgin: Brethren Press, 1976.

To walk humbly
by living as a servant people
who know the empowering love
exemplified by the basin and
towel.

10 THE POWER OF SERVANTHOOD

*The only 'superior' among
you is the one who serves
the others.*

JESUS OF NAZARETH

Now before the feast of the Passover, when Jesus knew that his hour had come to depart out of this world to the Father, having loved his own who were in the world, he loved them to the end. And during supper, when the devil had already put it into the heart of Judas Iscariot, Simon's son, to betray him, Jesus, knowing that the Father had given all things into his hands, and that he had come from God and was going to God, rose from supper, laid aside his garments, and girded himself with a towel. Then he poured water into a basin, and began to wash the disciples' feet, and to wipe them with the towel with which he was girded. He came to Simon Peter; and Peter said to him, "Lord, do you wash my feet?" Jesus answered him, "What I am doing you do not know now, but afterward you will understand." Peter said to him, "You shall never wash my feet." Jesus answered him, "If I do not wash you, you have no part in me." Simon Peter said to him, "Lord, not my feet only but also my hands and my head!" Jesus said to him, "He who has bathed does not need to wash, except for his feet, but he is clean all over; and you are clean, but not all of you." For he knew who was to betray him; that was why he said, "You are not all clean."

When he had washed their feet, and taken his garments, and resumed his place, he said to them, "Do you know what I have done to you? You call me Teacher and Lord; and you are right, for so I am. If I then, your Lord and Teacher, have washed your feet, you also ought to wash one another's feet. For I have given you an example, that you also should do as I have done to you. Truly, truly, I say to you, a servant is not greater than his master; nor is he who is sent greater than he who sent him. If you know these things, blessed are you if you do them.

John 13:1-17

Humility is just as much the opposite of self-abasement as it is of self-exaltation. To be humble is not to make comparisons. Secure in its reality, the self is neither better nor worse, bigger or smaller, than anything else in the universe. It is—is nothing, yet at the same time one with everything. It is in this sense that humility is absolute self-effacement.

To be nothing in the self-effacement of humility, yet, for the sake of the task, to embody its whole weight and importance in your bearing, as the one who has been called to undertake it. To give to people, works, poetry, art, what the self can contribute, and to take, simply and freely, what belongs to it by reason of its identity. Praise and blame, the winds of success and adversity, blow over such a life without leaving a trace or upsetting its balance.

Towards this, so help me, God—

Dag Hammarskjold
Markings

WHO WAS YOUR SERVANT at this time last year?" I remember being asked that question more than once when I have requested more than the person was prepared to do. And, I recall that some months ago, I was discussing a possible theme for an event related to a Council of Churches. I suggested that we focus upon the idea of Christians as a servant people. The Council executive was frank and direct: "That might appeal to a few Brethren, but the idea of being servants doesn't reach out and grab very many people."

I fear the Council executive is right. Madison Avenue can glamorize the most ugly hog, can even make Jello sound appetizing, but there is no cosmetic miracle for servanthood. One must have eyes for the rough beauty that is there and choose it, not for its glamour, but for its endurance and its sterling value.

Slaves and servants are passing from the world scene. We can hope that such roles will soon be entirely extinguished. In our own nation, machines do the work that servants once performed—machines and wives and husbands and children. We no longer think of servants in ordinary everyday life. The term "servant" may, then, have an archaic quality about it.

Servanthood bears a liability besides its archaic quality. That liability is its association with servitude and slavery. Howard Thurman, the black minister, teacher, and author, recalls the antipathy of his grandmother for the Apostle Paul and for his word to slaves. While Paul spoke of a new relationship between slaves and masters, he did not command an end to the system itself. Thurman's grandmother had been born a slave. She had cared for him as a boy, and his regular chore was to do all of her reading for her. She could neither read nor write. Two or three times a week, he read the Bible aloud to her. But she was very particular about what she heard. He could read the Psalms, some of Isaiah, and the Gospels, again and again. But the Pauline epistles, *never*. When he was in college, Howard Thurman asked his grandmother why she would not let him read from Paul.

"During the days of slavery," she said, "the master's minister would occasionally hold services for the slaves. Old man McGhee was so mean that he would not let a Negro minister preach to his slaves.

Blessed Are The Merciful
Good Samaritan
BRETHREN SERVICE COMMISSION
The Heifer Project
You Shall Love Your Neighbor As Yourself

Always, the white minister used a text from Paul. At least three or four times a year he used a text, 'Slaves, be obedient to those who are your earthly masters . . . as to Christ.' Then he would go on to show how it was God's will that we were slaves and how, if we were good and happy slaves, God would bless us. I promised my Maker that if I ever learned to read and if freedom ever came, I would not read that part of the Bible."

The image of servanthood does carry with it problems, particularly for those who have had such a status imposed upon them. For persons who may already feel oppressed by the world, it would be understandable if they chose other New Testament images for their discipleship, images such as "conquerors" or "a royal priesthood."

Still, we do find in common usage the term "public servant"—would that its embodiment were as common. And "service" is quite contemporary. The military uses it to describe the time served in the armed forces, considering it service to the nation. Those whose conscience will not sanction participation in war, seek an "alternative service." That is considered by Christians as service to God, but also as a service to the nation. And there are those service stations which dispense the increasingly rare petroleum products, and which in recent times have found it unnecessary to woo customers and, therefore, offer us a rather detached "self-service." These examples are sufficient to suggest that service, if not servanthood, has some current coinage.

What does it mean to offer service as a servant in our time? Is it to give the cup of cold water to the thirsty, break bread for the hungry, share clothing with the naked, bind the wounds of war victims in Southeast Asia?

Yes, surely, Christian servanthood involves all of these. We cannot see human need and pass by on the other side. But just as surely, servanthood must be more. Jesus was tempted in the wilderness to center his work in a relief ministry based upon physical need. That is one understanding of his temptation to turn stones into bread as reported in Luke's fourth chapter. Now, that was not such a bad idea. And he comes very close to centering upon a physical ministry when in Matthew 25 he says that, after all, the ones that truly worship me are those who offer drink, food, clothing and visitation. The power of the temptations was precisely because they were not evil in themselves; they were good; but they were partial. In the wilderness of decision, Jesus rejected a relief ministry as the norm of his servanthood.

Is servanthood, then, the doing of menial tasks, taking the job nobody else wants; washing the dishes after Sunday dinner; cleaning the floor after the dog makes a mess; arranging the chairs for the next meeting at church? Does the Last Supper support this view?

Yes, servanthood must involve a willingness to get one's hands dirty, seeing a dignity in all work and not just some work. But menial tasks alone are not the key to servanthood. Jesus did, amid an argument about greatness, do the job that servants usually do. But if you look at his entire ministry, it seems fair to say that the servanthood of Jesus was not one of just doing the menial jobs that were done by household servants. And certainly, one does not become a Christian servant by simply accepting all of the disagreeable and dirty jobs that may need to be done on behalf of the Church.

Servanthood is moving beyond the self to assume responsibility for others, to act and to do on behalf of others. That may involve physical relief. That may involve menial tasks. But more than these characteristics, are certain perspectives that are essential.

Being a servant people involves relinquishing rights. Such a perspective is embedded in the Philippian passage: "Have this mind among yourselves, which you have in Christ Jesus, who though he was in the form of God, did not count equality with God a thing to be grasped, but emptied himself, taking the form of a servant" (Philippians 2:7). Paul addresses us: "Think and act as did the Christ. He was equal to God, but he did not hold onto that position. Be willing to forego your position which is much less."

This is not an easy idea for our day. In the struggle for civil rights and for women's equality, as we have feebly identified with the dispossessed, we have emphasized the rights of every person. We have encouraged every person to insist upon the rights that are due to them, and to exercise those rights. There is a tension here with servanthood, but it needs to be understood that only the rights that are clearly established can be relinquished.

Though it is not an easy concept for our day, Christian servanthood has to do with not demanding our rights by social status, by occupational position, intellect or wealth. In other words, we do not depend upon out-ranking, out-arguing, or buying out the other person. Rather, "in the likeness of men," we affirm a common humanity with all.

Being a servant people means risking humiliation. That is the idea of the Incarnation: God risking humiliation at the hands of his creatures—"despised and rejected by men" (Isaiah 53:3). It is the ridiculousness of a Teacher washing his disciples' feet.

Our servanthood as persons, as a church, may ask us to stand humiliated and foolish in the eyes of the world. Sometimes we talk of humility, but humility is a tricky concept, for once you have pursued it, it has escaped. The least humble of all are those who self-consciously seek to display humility. But willingness to risk humiliation is for us an open possibility. It is the willingness to stand where faith and conviction demand, even when that may be costly to us in prestige and esteem.

Note, a servant people are not called to live in a state of humiliation, a state which would certainly not reflect wholeness. It is, rather, feeling and knowing from God such power within, that one can take the risk of humiliation for the sake of the Gospel.

Being a servant people means obedience. Is this not what Paul has in mind when he refers to himself, "Paul, a servant of Jesus Christ, called to be an apostle, set apart for the gospel of God . . . " (Romans 1:1). In being "set apart" one comes to obedience and regular disciplines. We are religiously casual in our age and much against disciplines. We are disenchanted with the traditional disciplines of the church, but we have not found new ones to take their place. Servanthood is obedience in daily living patterns and to visions.

A few years ago, a major commercial company distributed a booklet, "How to Retire at 35." The come-on title was not really an employment inducement, but, rather, spoke of that tragedy when men and women grow comfortable in their middle thirties and their forties and simply go through the motions in their work without zest and without real investment of self. They have stopped growing. They have retired from life.

The temptation to retire from life may be one of the most critical ones we face in an age when people complain of "burning out" and when growing numbers of people have retired from jobs. Servanthood speaks of obedience that gives structure to life and at the same time, strength and courage to respond to vision.

Being a servant people means having hope. The prophet of God, telling Israel about her role as the suffering servant, saw that present suffering in the light of future glory. Isaiah was not a defeatist prophet. He said, "he shall see the fruit of the travail of his soul and be satisfied" (Isaiah 53:11). Hope is experienced as a person joins in God's purpose. The hope does not presume a present Utopia, but does presume a coming kingdom. Servanthood brings hope because it is living in that kingdom.

The following chapter offers additional historical and biblical perspective on service.

CONCERNING THE JOHANNINE TEXT

The thirteenth chapter of John is often read to introduce the feetwashing service in the Church of the Brethren Love Feast. The feetwashing is called "the symbol of servanthood." There is another symbolism suggested in the text, and that is the symbolism of cleansing.

In the feetwashing, Jesus, as he often did, took everyday experiences and endowed them with religious meaning and significance. It was the custom for a slave or a servant to wash the feet of guests after they had traveled a distance. It was the custom which Jesus used to demonstrate his own servanthood and the need for a continual cleansing, even after baptism has been accomplished.

The time of the Last Supper is expressed in both *chronos* time— that is, "before the feast of the Passover," and *kairos* time—that is, "his hour had come."

After Jesus acts as servant, even insisting upon being servant to Peter, he commands that his example be imitated. The Brethren have understood that as a literal commandment not just for those disciples, but disciples for every age.

CONCERNING THE MARKINGS OF HUMILITY

The late Secretary General of the United Nations gives a clarification on humility, that it is neither self-abasement nor self-exaltation. Hammarskjold speaks of humility as not making comparisons. With humility there is a security that does not depend upon a favorable comparison to feel worthwhile.

Hammarskjold suggests that if we are truly humble, praise and blame and the winds of success and adversity will not upset our life balance.

A further consideration of the nature and meaning of humility will come in the final chapter.

FOR FURTHER CONSIDERATION

• Can the servant image be a commanding idea in a society where there are no servants in the usual sense of that term?

• Where in your community and in the world is the Church called to live as a servant people?

• In his study, *Power and Innocence,* the psychologist Rollo May notes that power is widely coveted, but rarely admitted in our society. Those who have power repress their awareness of it. He says, "Deeds of violence in our society are performed largely by those trying to establish their self-esteem, to defend their self-image, and to demonstrate that they, too, are significant." How do you assess May's observation that violence arises "out of powerlessness"? How is this related to servanthood and the relinquishing of power and rights?

• Is there a greater danger of retiring from life after one has retired from a vocation?

• Can you identify everyday customs or practices that come to embody religious meaning?

• The Church of the Brethren Annual Conference Statement on Brethren Service adopted in 1959, identified "three particularized ministries" as found in Greek terms, as expressions of the broad concerns of the Christian Church: *kerygma* (preaching, evangelism, and church extension), *koinonia* (fellowship, growth and nurture), and *diakonia* (helpfulness, service, and prophetic action). A helpful summary of service is given, saying that it is a faith expression

in unfaltering love and justice to all men and through helpful service toward all who are in need. It manifests the inseparability of faith and works. Each Christian who earnestly seeks the mind of Christ becomes concerned for every neighbor and for every neighborhood of the world. This concern encompasses the well-being of the whole man and the whole community of men. It includes both compassionate sharing with those in physical need and heroic action toward social justice. Inasmuch, as we serve even "these least," both individually and within the community, we serve our Lord and Master.

The entire statement provides a helpful understanding of the service to which we are called, and could provide a good resource for study.

SOME ACTIVITIES

Plan a service project for your class or congregation that deliberately involves manual labor.

In serving a dinner at the church, reverse the usual roles in food preparation, table setting and cleanup.

Volunteer for a custodial or maintenance task at some community institution.

Read Graham Greene's novel, *The Power and the Glory*, to see a whiskey priest acting as God's servant.

RESOURCES FOR ADDITIONAL STUDY

Brethren Life and Thought, Summer, 1958, and Autumn, 1968. Symposia on Brethren Volunteer Service.

Durnbaugh, Donald F. (Ed.). *To Serve the Present Age.* Elgin: Brethren Press, 1975.

Fey, Harold E. *Cooperation in Compassion: The Story of Church World Service.* New York: Friendship Press, 1966.

Keeney, William. *Lordship As Servanthood.* Scottdale, Pa.: Herald Press.

MacLeish, Archibald, *J. B.* New York: Houghton Mifflin, Co., 1958.

Slabaugh, Warren. *The Role of the Servant.* Elgin: Brethren Press, 1954.

Wirt, Sherwood Eliot. *Love Song: Augustine's Confessions for Modern Man.* New York: Harper-Row, 1971.

To walk humbly
by being in mission that lives
out mutuality.

11 THE OTHER SIDE OF SERVICE

Marriage is that relation between man and woman in which the independence is equal, the dependence mutual, and the obligation reciprocal.
LOUIS ANSPACHER

I do not pray for these only, but also for those who believe in me through their word, that they may all be one; even as thou, Father, art in me, and I in thee, that they also may be in us, so that the world may believe that thou hast sent me.

John 17:20, 21

So if there is any encouragement in Christ, any incentive of love, any participation in the Spirit, any affection and sympathy, complete my joy by being of the same mind, having the same love, being in full accord and of one mind. Do nothing from selfishness or conceit, but in humility count others better than yourselves. Let each of you look not only to his own interests, but also to the interests of others. Have this mind among yourselves, which you have in Christ Jesus, who, though he was in the form of God, did not count equality with God a thing to be grasped, but emptied himself, taking the form of a servant, being born in the likeness of men. And being found in human form he humbled himself and became obedient unto death, even death on a cross. Therefore God has highly exalted him and bestowed on him the name which is above every name, that at the name of Jesus every knee should bow, in heaven and on earth and under the earth, and every tongue confess that Jesus Christ is Lord, to the glory of God the Father.

Philippians 2:1-11

At the heart of the Bible and of Christian faith is Jesus Christ, Saviour and Lord, the suffering servant sent to earth by the Father to live and die and rise again for the liberation and salvation of all people (John 3). Jesus came as good news to the poor (Luke 4). His mission is the model for the church's mission, though we sometimes forget it and act as if this world's goods are meant to belong exclusively to some and not to all. We are members of one body and are related to each other (Romans 12). The church is the first fruits of a new humanity, a fellowship of mutual caring and concern (Galatians 5).

Missions practice in the past has sometimes made beggars out of brothers and sisters, as if the "sending" church were the rich man and the "receiving" church were Lazarus. The Holy Spirit will give guidance and correction if we reflect on our actions and seek a better way. What is needed now is a mutual mission in which the churches of Latin America and of the United States may minister to each other and to the world, each contributing according to the gifts given by Christ for the building up of the whole body in the unity of the Spirit in the bond of peace (Ephesians 4).

1978 Church of the Brethren Annual Conference General Board Report

IN THE TWO AND THREE-QUARTERS CENTURIES of history of the Church of the Brethren, service has been a persistent and dominating theme. Service colors our ethos. Being a servant people has been our calling. Service has been our body conditioner; it has been the protein of our diet; it has been the rote of our minds and the beat of our hearts.

There are some outward, visible signs of what service has meant to the Brethren. There is our liturgy in which we celebrate servanthood. We do it in the Love Feast, which is a re-enactment of the Last Supper, including the washing of feet, an obedience to a literal understanding of the word of Jesus, "If I then, your Lord and Teacher, have washed your feet, you also ought to wash one another's feet. For I have given you an example that you also should do as I have done to you" (John 13:14, 15).

There is a sign of our orientation toward service in the role of our church in the establishment of great ministries to human suffering, ministries that have emerged with ecumenical support, such as Heifer Project, CROP, Church World Service and the National Interreligious Board for Conscientious Objectors. Brethren Volunteer Service pioneered in the type of service that is now the Peace Corps and VISTA. In the research related to the establishment of the Peace Corps by the Kennedy Administration, there was material contributed by those who had been in Brethren Volunteer Service.

It is true that in the whole Christian family, the various religious bodies respond to particular images and themes in our sacred writings, our histories, and our heritages. The Brethren have been drawn by the image of the servant, while others have taken more inspiration from such images as priest or evangelist or shepherd. We have those images, also, but it is the servant image that has captivated our people. The most eloquent and poetic expression of the servant idea comes from the prophet Isaiah in what is called "the Suffering Servant" passage:

> He was despised and rejected by men;
> a man of sorrows and acquainted with grief;
> and as one from whom men hide their faces
> he was despised, and we esteemed him not.
>
> Surely he has borne our griefs and carried
> our sorrows; yet we esteemed him stricken,
> smitten by God and afflicted.
>
> Isaiah 53:3, 4

From these verses, commented Graydon Snyder, Dean of Bethany Theological Seminary in *In His Hand,* Part 2, and from the remaining verses of Isaiah 52:13 through 53:12, "we understand the mission of Jesus, and even more important, from (them) we understand the nature of the Christian Church."

The servant meaning comes from Jesus, himself, as he apparently identifies his own ministry with the suffering servant of Israel. He set forth his purpose, "The Son of man came not to be served but to serve, and to give his life as a ransom for many" (Matthew 20:28). In the Upper Room, dramatically and astonishingly, he assumed the role of the servant, washing the disciples' feet (John 13:1-20).

The servant image is used freely by Paul and other New Testament writers to describe Jesus. In the Philippian passage above, for example, Paul says of the Master, that he "emptied himself, taking the form of a servant, being born in the likeness of men." It is also used to describe the way of Christians as when Peter admonishes, "live as servants of God" (1 Peter 2:16).

In our history and in that part of scripture to which we respond most readily, the ideal of service has been a goal, a vision and an imperative. It has tremendous appeal to us. It is true that we are far from embodying fully the servant image. We need a continual reminder of that ministry. Yet, if the Church is not conscious of servanthood, it is just below consciousness. Service is both necessary and urgent in being the people of God.

But there is another side to service. There is a side that has remained in the shadows for us. The other side is the side of being served — not demanding service, but of willingness to be served. It is taking the time and caring about being mutual in our service, in our mission as the people of God.

My home is but a short distance from the campus of the University of La Verne. My wife, Pat, and I often walk through the campus late in the afternoon or early evening, on our way to play tennis on the college courts. Recently, I have reflected upon how peaceful seems this place— this idyllic and calm setting of a small college. I am aware that in other quarters it would not seem so peaceful. La Verne, as other small colleges, wages a frantic effort to get the bills paid and to discover its own role and place in higher education and its relationship to the church, nevertheless outwardly, the campus has a beautiful calm.

How different that feeling is from the college campuses of a decade ago. It seems a generation past, but it was just over a decade ago that we were reading of a new president at Columbia University, trying to gain control of that institution. Columbia, located on Manhattan, but just a brick's throw from Harlem, was one of the first to feel the disruption instigated by radical students with an attack upon the school's ties with the military establishment. When the turmoil persisted, the president of Columbia, a man in his early sixties, resigned. The trustees sought a younger person with the energy and the insight to cope with the problems. Borrowing time to find the person they really wanted, the trustees hastily turned to an interim, acting president. The man to whom they turned to cool the campus was their Dean of the School of International Affairs. He was Andrew Cordier. Cordier had been a history professor at Manchester College, but when the United Nations was born, he became the Assistant to the Secretary General and continued in that position through all the early years of the United Nations, even into U Thant's administration.

Cordier has since died. At the time he came to Columbia's Acting Presidency, he was nearly seventy. In him, the trustees had found their young man, and they soon changed his title from Acting President to President. His ability to deal constructively with that situation was in the way he related to students. He listened to them. He went to their student rallies. He invited them as guests to his home. He gave them an opportunity to contribute to the solution.

The very same year that the Brethren adopted a statement on service, Andrew Cordier spoke at the Annual Conference. This was ten years before the Columbia presidency, and revealed a perspective that would later help him re-establish order at Columbia. His speech dealt with the special responsibility we have as Americans because of our great wealth and our vast development. Then he moved to the dilemma posed for us in that very fact. He said,

> We have spent much more time on the philosophy of giving in the Western world than we have on the problems of receiving. One of the problems we are running into in the African-Asian states is just that. "It is," said one prime minister recently, "very difficult for us to receive." Receiving has been associated too often historically with ignominy of weakness, of helplessness, and even of inferiority.

In the years since that speech, I have often thought about Cordier's words. Why has the Western world, and why have we in the Christian community so emphasized giving and serving, that receiving and being served are a problem? *That is the other side of service.* It is not simply modern or Western or Christian as a problem. It is a human problem. It is reflected from the time of Jesus, when in the Upper Room, Peter is aghast that he would be served by Jesus. Remember how Jesus met that protest, saying to Peter, "Unless you let me serve you, you can really have no part in me" (Paraphrase, John 13:8). When we cut ourselves off from being served, when the other person cannot give us anything, then we have no relationship with that person. (Small wonder that in the new *Pastor's Manual* for our church, the meanings of the feetwashing service, which are listed, include not only cleansing and service, but also an understanding that it is "an act of being served." The Manual declares that the ritual recognizes the instrument of our renewal can be the service performed by some brother or sister.)

Peter was not alone. The other disciples had difficulty in being served, or even in seeing Jesus served. There is the story of the service of a woman who anointed Jesus with some costly ointment. To the disciples, it was a scandal—it was the poor who should be served, not Jesus. But Jesus received her service. He did not call it a waste as did the disciples; he said, "She has done a beautiful thing to me" (Mark 14:3-9).

The other side of service is reflected, also, in personal experience. Nancy Poling and her family now live in Northern Illinois, but they were recently residents of California and members of the La Verne congregation. When Nancy was still my near neighbor, she spoke to me of a friend she had in Pennsylvania and of the problem that friendship posed to her. This was what Nancy said of her friend, as I recall:

> I probably felt closer to her than to any friend I have ever had, except my husband. We spent a lot of time together, taking our pre-schoolers to the library and for summer picnics.
>
> But after a few years, I began to feel that something was missing in our relationship. What could be wrong, I thought, when I had such a giving friend, such a thoughtful friend? She was always there when I felt troubled by the hassles of young motherhood. She was always glad to keep my kids for me if the need arose. She was always concerned and caring.
>
> I discovered what was wrong. There was nothing I could do for her. Her own four children never seemed to get the best of her. She never shared her own needs, needs to get away from the kids, needs for an occasional emotional crutch, needs for comfort. She never even needed to borrow an egg or a cup of sugar.
>
> I knew what was wrong. There was nothing I could give her.

Nancy concluded that a friendship would likely not survive when one person is denied the joy of giving. And as I listened to Nancy, I identified with her, knowing persons and situations who always give, but seem never able to receive from me. It is a barrier to our relationship.

In the Church, we occasionally have persons who seem to feel they are suited only to leadership and speaking roles. They participate only if they are giving. *I have come to feel that listening is one of the qualifications for speaking in the Church.* Those who can be served by the spoken word have a basis for serving by speaking. "The other side of service" is a factor in marriage relationships. In the traditional roles, the husband served the marriage by providing the economic and physical security. The wife served the marriage by personal services to the family. She fixed the meals and prepared the clothes for her husband. She made him comfortable when he arrived home. They both served the marriage, but theirs was a very different kind of service. Except for minor courtesies, such as opening the door and holding the coat, the husband never gave personal services. The wife was always giving personal services, but may have felt that she was never being served. And the husband did not experience that opportunity for giving personal service. Our marriage relationship will surely be enriched if we give attention to both serving and being served.

The other side of service. The servant image must continue as a strong motif in our vision. We must discover and develop an equal vision of being served. Not a demand for service, rather, an openness to service. It is the openness to receive another person. It is openness to God. The mission factor for the people of God is a mutual mission.

CONCERNING THE JOHANNINE TEXT

The brief passage from John is from what is often called "The High Priestly Prayer" of Jesus. Read the entire prayer from Chapter 17, verses 1-26. There is a sequence in the prayer from prayer for the Son, himself, to those who are his immediate followers, to the Church universal, "that they may all be one." It is the last part of the prayer that has become a dominant theme in the ecumenical church.

Note the content of each part of the prayer. For himself: that he may face the time that is at hand in a way that will glorify God, and that he may act so that he may offer eternal life. For his immediate disciples: the revealing of God through Jesus, the living and working of the disciples in the world, the unity of the disciples, that the joy of Jesus Christ will be in them, that they may be protected from evil, being dedicated to truth, sending the disciples into the world. For the Church Universal: that there may be unity so that the world might believe in Jesus Christ.

CONCERNING THE PHILIPPIAN TEXT

The servanthood of Jesus Christ is beautifully told by Paul in the Philippian passage. With regard to that servanthood, we are to be "of the same mind." In such a mindset, we complete the joy of Christ and know our greatest joy. Interestingly, Paul's argument on behalf of joy is to avoid the power struggles, to avoid doing things from motives of selfishness and conceit.

The paradoxical nature of the Gospel is here revealed, in that the one who "emptied himself" is the very One God exalts until "every knee should bow, in heaven and on earth and under the earth . . . " There is an expectation that ultimately every human "tongue will confess that Jesus Christ is Lord . . . "

CONCERNING MUTUAL MISSION

The excerpt from the Church of the Brethren General Board report is taken from the central part of the paper headed, "Biblical Imperatives." It comes after a review of Church of the Brethren relationships in Latin America over the past thirty years and of the current situation in that part of the world, emphasizing our common tradition with Christianity. After the quoted section, the General Board sets forth two program emphases that are to be based upon mutuality. One is to involve a partner church in Latin America and carries the Spanish title, Misión Mutua en las Américas. The second involves Hispanic ministries in the United States and Puerto Rico. Through these ministries, the church seeks to embody and express the principle of mutuality in mission.

FOR FURTHER CONSIDERATION

• Identify the difference between demanding service and being willing to be served.

• In seeking mutual relationships, how can initiatives be taken?

• What are the special considerations in offering mutual service when those involved are a teacher and pupils? Employer and employees? Pastor and people?

• In serving and being served, it is important to avoid the necessity of a tit-for-tat arrangement—that is, at times you may serve one person, but be served by another person. Every relationship does not require complete equality.

• It has been said that a way to develop a deeper friendship is to ask the friend to do something for you that can easily be done. Do you agree with that observation?

• Can you think of times that Jesus permitted others to offer him service? Is your service to Jesus Christ mutual?

• Are there parts of the Christian church for whom you have difficulty in praying a prayer of unity? From what parts do you feel most distant?

SOME ACTIVITIES

Write to the Church of the Brethren General Board to secure the latest report on "Mutual Mission in the Americas." Identify the values you see coming from this mission program.

Read as a unison reading the Philippians passage at the beginning of this chapter. Or, ask one person to read the passage while others follow a person who leads the group in giving body movements that are expressive of the words.

Encourage your congregation to develop a mutual mission with another congregation, if possible with a congregation of ethnic minority people.

List the times when you have received or have been served and felt comfortable with accepting without repayment.

RESOURCES FOR ADDITIONAL STUDY

de Castillejo, Irene. *Knowing Woman: A Feminine Psychology*. New York: Harper-Row, 1974.

Illich, Ivan. *Tools for Conviviality*. New York: Harper-Row, 1974.

Marty, Martin E. *The Search for a Usable Future*. New York: Harper-Row, 1969.

O'Connor, Elizabeth. *Eighth Day of Creation*. Waco, Texas: Word Books, 1971.

Southard, Samuel. *People Need People*. Crawfordsville, Ind.: Westminster, 1970.

Thurman, Howard. *The Search for Common Ground*. New York: Harper-Row, 1971.

To walk humbly
  by celebrating the Lordship of
  Christ and the interdependence
  of all humanity.

12   OF DIVINE
AND
HUMAN
BONDING

Around Your table, Lord, we come,
Hearts hungering for You,
And, as we eat, please feed our
    souls
With fellowship that's true.

MARY SUE ROSENBERGER

I am the true vine, and my Father is the vinedresser. Every branch of mine that bears no fruit, he takes away, and every branch that does bear fruit he prunes, that it may bear more fruit. You are already made clean by the word which I have spoken to you. Abide in me and I in you. As the branch cannot bear fruit by itself, unless it abides in the vine, neither can you, unless you abide in me. I am the vine, you are the branches. He who abides in me, and I in him, he it is that bears much fruit, for apart from me you can do nothing. If a man does not abide in me, he is cast forth as a branch and withers; and the branches are gathered, thrown into the fire and burned. If you abide in me, and my words abide in you, ask whatever you will, and it shall be done for you. By this my Father is glorified, that you bear much fruit, and so prove to be my disciples. As the Father has loved me, so have I loved you; abide in my love. If you keep my commandments, you will abide in my love, just as I have kept my Father's commandments and abide in his love. These things I have spoken to you, that my joy may be in you, and that your joy may be full.

John 15:1-11

It really boils down to this: that all life is inter-related. We are all caught in an inescapable network of mutuality, tied into a single garment of destiny. Whatever affects one directly, affects all indirectly. We are made to live together because of the inter-related structure of reality. Did you ever stop to think that you can't leave for your job in the morning without being dependent on most of the world? You get up in the morning and go to the bathroom and reach over for the sponge, and that's handed to you by a Pacific Islander. You reach for a bar of soap, and that's given to you at the hands of a Frenchman. And then you go into the kitchen to drink your coffee for the morning, and that's poured into your cup by a South American. And maybe you want tea: that's poured into your cup by a Chinese. Or maybe you're desirous of having cocoa for breakfast, and that's poured into your cup by a West African. And then you reach over for your toast, and that's given to you at the hands of an English-speaking farmer, not to mention the baker. And before you finish eating breakfast in the morning, you've depended on more than half of the world. This is the way our universe is structured, this is its inter-related quality. We aren't going to have peace on earth until we recognize this basic fact of the inter-related structure of all reality.

Now let me say, secondly, that if we are to have peace in the

world, men and nations must embrace the nonviolent affirma-
tion that ends and means must cohere.

Martin Luther King, Jr.
The Trumpet of Conscience

WORDS FORMED BY MARTIN NIEMÖLLER have for years been a reminder to me that my life and my destiny are interwoven with my
brothers and sisters. Niemöller was born in Germany and during World
War I, became a U-boat commander. After that war, a troubled young
man decided to enter the ministry. During his university days of
preparation, Germany was experiencing political turbulence. Niemöller
was attracted to the ultra conservative elements who were seeking control of the coalition government. It seemed to him to be the best defense
against the Communists and could bring a more favorable relationship
between the church and the state.

Not long after Niemöller's ordination, the National Socialist party
began to rise in power. He supported the party in 1924 and 1928. He
and many other pastors endorsed the basic goals of National Socialism.
One of those goals was especially appealing, the Nazis declaring: "We
demand freedom for all religious confessions within the state, insofar as
they are not a danger to it and do not offend the moral feelings of the
German race. The party as such stands for positive Christianity." When
Adolf Hitler became chancellor in 1933, Martin Niemöller believed that
it was for the good of the nation and the church.

Niemöller was mistaken. As the Nazi government began to sup-
press freedom, Niemöller's protest was heard from the pulpit. The
dreaded Gestapo harassed him and then, in 1937, arrested him. He
became Hitler's "personal prisoner." He was offered freedom if he
would leave the ministry, but he refused. He remained in prison until
the end of World War II, and in his last days of confinement, was await-
ing execution.

This is the background that gives perspective to a statement given
to the Council of the Evangelical Church in Germany in 1945:

In Germany, the Nazis first came for the Communists, and I
didn't speak up because I was not a Communist.

Then they came for the Jews, and I did not speak up because I
was not a Jew.

Then they came for the Trade Unionists, and I didn't speak up
because I wasn't a Trade Unionist.

Then they came for the Catholics, and I was a Protestant so I
didn't speak up.

> Then they came for ME . . . by that time there was no one to speak up for any one.

Niemöller's statement, with its tragic reality in the background, drives home to us our inter-relatedness. An injustice afflicting one person is a threat to every other person. Discrimination against some is potential discrimination against all. The safety of the majority lies in the security of the minority. The erosion of rights for any minority is a cancer which tears at the life of every citizen. The Brethren, who are few in number, who have acted like a minority, and who often find themselves a minority voice as one "crying in the wilderness," should be especially sensitive to the rights of all persons and groups. Our own history shows how the state can become oppressive when we do not give to Caesar what Caesar demands.

That our destiny is related to the destiny of the rest of humanity is not a new idea. The Hebrews had a sense of salvation of the people. Theirs was not a faith which pointed toward the saving of individual souls, all unrelated. Our salvation depends upon what is happening to our brothers and our sisters. Jesus suggests that we cannot fully give ourselves to God as long as we are unreconciled to those around us (Matthew 5:23, 24). In being the disciples of Jesus, we are not only to witness to an Ethiopian riding by (Acts 8:26-40), not only to instruct a Priscilla so that she may instruct (Acts 18:24-28), but we are to "make disciples of all nations" (Matthew 28:19). *Nations!*

It is becoming increasingly clear that our redemption is related not alone to other humans. We are inter-related with the whole of creation. As we destroy a part of our environment, a part of us is destroyed, until finally, if we destroy our environment, we destroy ourselves.

We are inter-related with all of creation in ways that are mysterious and which we do not begin to understand. A positive thought has power going out from it that can give encouragement to another person. On the other hand, our negative intentions toward others can have an adverse effect on them, though I do not believe it has the power to control them. In ways we do not understand, our lives touch others even when we are not physically present with them. This helps to explain the power of intercessory prayer. It does make a difference when we pray for other people, our prayer directed Godward, redirected by God to those persons.

Our interdependence is with all humanity. One of the forms in which this interdependence is found is male-female. That interdependence has always been present. It was required for the propagation of the species. It was found in complementary roles assumed in life by males and females, roles in which the male traditionally assumed responsibility to "head" the household.

While women have always contributed to the whole of life in a major way (the names of Sarah, Esther, Ruth, and Mary are witnesses to such in ancient times), and while a few women and a few men have always gone beyond the rigid male-female role definitions of their age, the women's movement of the past decade is bringing a fundamental restructuring of society. The old definitions of what was the work of men and what was the work of women is being challenged. Women are a part of the employed work force as never before. It is now recognized as a matter of justice that women are to receive equal pay as men for equal work. While this is recognized, we are far from achieving it.

In the Church of the Brethren, we have committed ourselves to equality for women. All of the positions of the Church are open to men and women alike. Yet, we are slow to elect women to our highest offices and while increasing numbers of women are preparing for ministry, congregations are not readily accepting women in the role of pastor.

The most serious Bible study that has been done in the last decade has been around the women's issue. We have become aware of feminine images of God, as well as masculine. It is much clearer that God is not literally male; that male language usually associated with God is metaphor. We have discovered the cultural context of Paul's writings about women and the complexity of what he did say—on the one hand saying women should remain silent in the church; on the other, giving instructions to women when they prophesy. There are many good books on the relationship of male and female from a biblical perspective, but the one I have found most helpful is Virginia Ramey Mollenkott's *Women, Men and the Bible*. In her book, she contrasts the "Christian way of relating" with the "carnal way of relating." Depending upon the way Jesus interacted with women and the Pauline epistles, Mollenkott concludes that the Christian way is one of mutual submission—not domination by either male or female. She contrasts this with "the carnal pattern of dominance and submission . . . " In one of the last chapters, Mollenkott offers five principles for interpreting scripture that can be helpful in studying the Bible for any reason:

1. Try to grasp the literal meaning of a passage as it was probably understood at the time of its first writing.

2. Pay attention to the point of view in the passage.

3. When we are reading dialogue, it is important to ask ourselves such questions as these: What is the tone of the various individual speakers? Are they angry with one another, or are they on good terms? Is one trying to trap the other? If so, is the answer given affected by the attitude of the questioner?

4. No matter what passage we are reading, it is important to ask ourselves about the literary form in which the ideas are cast.

5. Above all, place the passage in context.

We could begin with creation and by being attuned to the various elements in creation discover our inter-relatedness and our dependence upon each other. For the Christian, the beginning is not with creation, but with the Creator. "In the beginning God . . . " We know we are related by knowing we come from a common source. *It is in Jesus Christ that we most discover God's intention for all of creation.* We discover God's intention from the natural order, from other people, including great teachers and leaders, from our own intuition and emotions and reasoning. But our greatest revelation comes from Jesus Christ. Two things happen to us as Jesus Christ becomes a dominant influence in our lives. First, we fulfill the Creator's intention for our lives, and, second, we come into a proper relationship with the rest of creation.

Worship is the first and primary way that we become "in Jesus Christ." Worship, as Isaiah discovered, is that activity in which an awareness comes of our own condition: "Woe is me! For I am lost; for I am a man of unclean lips, and I dwell in the midst of a people of unclean lips; for my eyes have seen the King, the Lord of hosts!" Worship is that activity in which we feel newly created: "Behold this has touched your lips; your guilt is taken away, and your sin forgiven." Worship is that activity in which we are apprehended and sent: "And I heard the voice of the Lord saying, 'Whom shall I send, and who will go for us?' Then I said, "Here I am! Send me." (Quotations from Isaiah are from Chapter 6, verses 5, 7, and 8.)

As we worship, we discover an interdependence with God, with whom we become co-creators, that is, God does become dependent upon us, making the Divine appeal through us and achieving the Divine purpose through us. Our dependence upon God is acknowledged in the very act of worship. We discover an interdependence with "the earth and the heavens" (Genesis 2:4) for whom we have responsibility as those who have dominion (Genesis 1:26), that is, created in the image of God, because of our special place in creation, we are to exercise a stewardship of created life on behalf of God. And we depend upon the elements of that creation for our own physical sustenance. We discover an interdependence with other people, who become to us neighbors. The second breath of worship inhales the neighbor, "You shall love your neighbor as yourself" (Mark 12:31). And the crucial question becomes not "Who is my neighbor?" but who "proved neighbor?" (Luke 10:36). We have no meaning and no salvation apart from the neighbor.

There is yet another relationship that comes in worship. It is in worship that we discover our interdependence with the past and the future. From the past we draw the substance of worship, and toward the future we are called, as in the faith of Abraham who "obeyed when he was called to go out to a place which he was to receive as an inheritance; and he went out, not knowing where he was to go" (Hebrews 11:8). That is, we are dependent upon all of our fathers and mothers in the faith who have borne to us a faith from both the Old Covenant and the New Covenant and have brought to us the Church as our spiritual legacy. They were dependent upon us and we upon those in the future to give meaning within this world to what we do.

A definition or a description of worship may be helpful. *Worship is a recalling of God's action in history, in the history of God's people, and in our own personal experience. It is remembering the promises of God and the fulfillment of those promises. It is anticipation of God's intended action and preparation to be a part of that activity. It is a celebration of past and present reality and future hope. It is an exploration of God's will for our lives, for the lives of all of God's people, and for the world. Worship is the centering or focusing experience of the people of God and for the individual.* The substance of worship is the Word of God (the Word of God is not identical with scripture but is consistent with the scripture, so that preaching and teaching are a part of worship, as well as sources besides the Bible). The attitude of worship is prayer. The mood of worship is celebration. And the language of worship is music.

Our bonding with God and with all creation is cemented in the celebration of worship. We celebrate the One who has created us. And we celebrate the unity we know with the earth and with other creatures. We celebrate our diversity which is the strength of our interdependence and which Paul illustrates forcefully as he uses the metaphor of the human body to describe the Church. And we celebrate our solidarity. To be a genuinely cementing experience, the celebrants must enter into drama of worship, forsaking the role of dispassionate critic. In his book, *The Feast of Fools,* Harvey Cox gives understanding to the nature of the celebrative experience when he says, "Celebration demands a kind of unselfconscious participation that prevents our analyzing it while it is happening. If we begin analyzing our experience of festivity during a celebration, we stop celebrating—and the object of our examination vanishes." So,

> Make a joyful noise to God,
>   all the earth;
> sing the glory of his name;
> give to him glorious praise!
> *Psalm 66:1, 2*

CONCERNING THE JOHANNINE TEXT

There are many images, or metaphors, in the New Testament that give understanding to what it means to be a Christian and to the nature of the Church. Those in the Church are the saints, the servants, the disciples, the believers. They form a royal priesthood. They are a chosen nation. They are the followers of the Way. These metaphors, saying that the Christian is like something else that is familiar, burst with meaning and new understanding of what it means to live as a Christian.

One of those metaphors comes in the agricultural scene of the vineyard. It is an image chosen from everyday life. They have just eaten the bread and have drunk wine together. Did the wine remind Jesus of the vineyard as an image? Was there a vine growing beneath that Upper Room and climbing up and through the window? Did he see a vine on the way to Gethsemane? In any case, he uses the vine in an allegory to describe the Church. It is an allegory because it has material form that has corresponding parts in an abstract or spiritual meaning. That is, the vineyard has different parts that represent different parts in the sphere of the Divine and the human.

There are three parts to the allegory of the vineyard: the vine, the branches, and the vinedresser. As Jesus chooses the vine as part of his own self-image, he identifies with Israel. The vine was a common metaphor for the Jewish nation. In reference to the Exodus, the Psalmist says,

> Thou didst bring a vine out of Egypt;
> thou didst drive out the nations and plant it.
> *Psalm 80:8*

The vine was used as an emblem of Israel under the Maccabees in the second century before Christ, and appeared on the coins of the time. Often a vine with grapes would be in a carving over the main door of the synagogue. The Jewish historian, Josephus, described the doors of the Temple at Jerusalem as being under a great golden vine. The prophets often used the figure of the vine to say that Israel is a vine that has gone bad—not producing the fruit God has intended (see Jeremiah 2:21 and Isaiah 5:7, for example). It is in this context that Jesus says, "I am the *true* vine . . . "

The branches are the Church. They are an organic whole with the vine. Jesus speaks of the relationship between the two, concluding that we prove to be his disciples if we bear much fruit. Then he turns to themes of love and joy. The Christian can experience and bear the fruit of the Spirit only if in dynamic and flowing relationship to Christ. There are those who see the joy, the peace, the fellowship that is in Jesus Christ, but want to achieve those on their own. But when we try to do it on our own, then we find a withering and dying.

God is pictured as the vinedresser, whose central purpose is tending the vines and the branches. Feeding and pruning, everything is done, to bring the whole vine to its fulfillment. Implied in the figure of the vinedresser is a cultivation of existing power. The vinedresser does not seek dates or oranges from the vines, but seeks that fruit which is native to each branch. And the vinedresser cares for each branch as a living thing. Faithfulness is the test—not color, not shape, not wood, but fruit. Jesus talks about the cutting away of branches that bear no fruit. That trimming of "dead wood" is not something which a live branch does to a dead branch. No, it is the vinedresser who does the trimming. Even the productive branches are pruned that they may bear more fruit. In the vineyard, there is a disciplining, a keeping in spiritual trim.

CONCERNING OUR INTERRELATEDNESS

Martin Luther King, Jr., illustrates our daily interrelatedness and dependence upon peoples all over the world, and then warns that peace will never come "until we recognize this basic fact of the interrelated structure of all reality." He calls for means and ends to cohere. Church historian Martin E. Marty has said that "The great need of our time is for coherences." He cites the threat of incoherence and asks for order, purpose and pattern. (*Christian Century*, October 17, 1979, pp. 996, 997) In such coherence is the hope of wholeness for the person and unity for the entire creation.

FOR FURTHER CONSIDERATION

• Where in our society is injustice creating victims that is a threat to all of us?

• Think about ways in which we can achieve unity while affirming diversity. What are implications to us of diversity in personalities, in abilities, in interests, in philosophies, in faiths?

• Are there any roles, aside from reproductive, that are inherently or essentially male or female?

• Consider your own experience of worship. Identify the times when you most experience worship. Read the sixth chapter of Isaiah and discuss the whole of Isaiah's vision.

• In your morning worship service, note the elements of worship that celebrate "the Lordship of Christ and the interdependence of all humanity."

• Relate the allegory from the vineyard with those who are not of the Body of Christ.

SOME ACTIVITIES

Write a prayer which acknowledges and expresses thanksgiving for Jesus Christ, including as many different forms of relationship as you can.

Study your congregation's organization over the past five years. List the various positions, such as Minister, Moderator, Church Board, commissions, ushers, church school teachers, youth advisors, and put beside them the names of those who have served. Evaluate whether all parts of your congregation, men and women, young and old, various ethnic backgrounds, are represented in the leadership. Are there any positions you feel inappropriate to be filled by a man? by a woman? by a youth? by an older person? Why?

Review your dependence upon peoples of other nations in your experience of today. Make a list and compare it with the list of others in a class or with someone you ask to share the exercise.

RESOURCES FOR ADDITIONAL STUDY

Berdyaev, Nicolas. *The Destiny of Man*. New York: Harper-Row, 1961.

Cox, Harvey. *The Feast of Fools*. Cambridge, Mass.: Harvard University Press, 1969.

Keohane, Robert O. and Nye, Joseph S. *Power and Interdependence: World Politics in Transition*. Waltham, Mass.: Little, 1977.

McHale, John. *The Future of the Future*. New York: Braziller, 1969.

Mollenkott, Virginia. *Women, Men and the Bible*. Nashville: Abingdon, 1977.

Morse, Kenneth I. *Move In Our Midst*. Elgin: Brethren Press, 1977.

13 WHAT GOD REQUIRES

If I am a Christian, I must do my best to realize Christian truth in the social as well as in the personal life.

NICOLAS BERDYAEV

With what shall I come before the Lord,
  and bow myself before God on high?
Shall I come before him with burnt offerings,
  with calves a year old?
Will the Lord be pleased with thousands of rams,
  with ten thousands of rivers of oil?
Shall I give my first-born for my transgression,
  the fruit of my body for the sin of my soul?"
He has showed you, O man, what is good;
  and what does the Lord require of you
but to do justice, and to love kindness,
  and to walk humbly with your God?
                                    Micah 6:6-8

God of grace and God of glory, On Thy people pour Thy power;
Crown Thine ancient church's story; Bring her bud to glorious flower.
Grant us wisdom, Grant us courage, For the facing of this hour,
  For the facing of this hour.

Lo! the hosts of evil round us Scorn Thy Christ, assail His ways!
Fear and doubts too long have bound us, Free our hearts to work and
  praise.
Grant us wisdom, Grant us courage, For the living of these days,
  For the living of these days.

Cure Thy children's warring madness, Bend our pride to Thy control;
Shame our wanton, selfish gladness, Rich in things and poor in soul.
Grant us wisdom, Grant us courage, Lest we miss Thy kingdom's goal,
  Lest we miss Thy kingdom's goal.

Set our feet on lofty places; Gird our lives that they may be
Armored with all Christlike graces In the fight to set men free.
Grant us wisdom, Grant us courage, That we fail not man nor Thee!
  That we fail not man nor Thee!

Save us from weak resignation To the evils we deplore;
Let the search for Thy salvation Be our glory evermore.
Grant us wisdom, Grant us courage, Serving Thee whom we adore,
  Serving Thee whom we adore. Amen.
                                    Harry Emerson Fosdick

A S WE COME TO CONCLUDE this part of our study of Goals for the 80s,
  we might ask the distinctive character of these goals. Certainly, the
goals statement (see beginning pages) is unique in the way it has used a
verse from scripture as an outline for several emphases. The statement

is also unique in its admonition to seek the guidance of the Holy Spirit and to study prayerfully certain chapters of the Bible. By listing entire chapters and by seeking the Holy Spirit, the statement obviously intends an openness to discovery, an explosiveness in the process, rather than a narrow, limited focus on a specific theme.

In the content itself, how could this statement be distinguished from one we might have adopted in the 1940's or the 1950's? I think one sees in the statement more attention to creation and to the global community, than we might have observed at an earlier time. Earlier eras in the church would have spoken of the simple life; this time, the term "lifestyles" is employed. And there is considerable emphasis upon wholeness and mutuality among the peoples of the world, within the church, and within the person. Certainly, this is not a statement of the solitary Christian concerned only for individual salvation; in almost every line of the goals, there is a corporateness, a sense of the faith community and a relationship to all of humanity.

Of all the distinguishing features of the statement, however, I believe the most obvious is its focus upon justice. The statement leaps out at us with the call "to do justice" That is the first call. And the theme of justice can be felt vibrating through the entire statement. The Brethren have been one of the "three historic peace churches," a condition now being enhanced by a "New Call to Peacemaking," involving us with the Friends and Mennonites who share that heritage with us. Peace is with us a consuming passion, probably that feature of our history for which we are best known. Our commitment to peace becomes an issue whenever discussions of merger are on the agenda and almost always when we give testimony to government. While the entire Church of the Brethren is more diverse in its views of peace than would have been true in earlier times, the official position and the leadership of the church have never been stronger in renouncing war and war making and in being peace-makers. Peace is related to justice. Indeed, war always denies and destroys justice. There will not be justice until peace is realized. But peace and justice are distinct and different emphases and the element that is distinctive in the Annual Conference goals statement is justice.

The Brethren have been a people of compassion who have responded to human need. It has often been observed that across the whole membership the one thing that the Brethren want to do is to feed the hungry. World hunger has been a natural concern for a people who have been rural and who have settled on some of the richest farmland in the world. When appeals are made across our denomination, we generally respond most generously to the one for hunger needs. Heifer Project International is an agency given birth within our church because it caught the imagination and the vision of the Brethren. Of ecumenical agencies, we have probably supported most enthusiastically those which have responded to hunger such as CROP and Church World Service. Hunger and justice are related. As long as some are hungry while others are fed, justice is not present. But hunger and justice are distinct and different emphases and what is distinctive in the Annual Conference Goals statement is justice.

In the Goals for the 80s, as in the Micah text, justice is linked with "to love tenderly" and "to walk humbly."

JUSTICE

There are at least three ways in which justice is used in scripture. In the Micah passage it means to do what is fair. That is, there is a special obligation to give what is due to the other person and to avoid taking what does not belong to you. Those who are unjust "covet fields, and seize them; and houses, and take them away; they oppress a man and his house, a man and his inheritance" (Micah 2:2).

A second major meaning of biblical justice is that of making things right. It is a part of the messianic expectation when

> Every valley shall be lifted up,
> and every mountain and hill be made low;
> the uneven ground shall become level,
> and the rough places a plain.
> *Isaiah 40:4*

The Prince of Peace will come, and it is then that things will be made right, "with justice and with righteousness from this time forth and forevermore" (Isaiah 9:7). Such a reordering is found in the Magnificat (Luke 1:46-55) and in the Isaiah passage with which Jesus identifies at Nazareth (Luke 4:16-21, Isaiah 61:1-2). Things that are wrong are made right. The poor hear good news. The captives are released. The blind see. The oppressed are liberated. The word of the Lord is proclaimed. In Revelation, this justice is seen in a vision of things to come in a new heaven and a new earth when God "will wipe away every tear from their eyes, and death shall be no more, neither shall there be mourning nor crying nor pain any more, for the former things have passed away" (Revelation 21:4).

The Christian is to make things right as an instrument of the Divine purpose. This goes beyond doing what is fair in your own personal dealings; it takes responsibility for justice for the whole human family.

A third use of justice is a theological understanding of the incarnation. That is, a holy God would be just in condemning humanity because of sinfulness. But God's justice is accompanied by love, and God, therefore, sends his Son to pay the penalty for our sin. Justice is achieved through the punishment, not of the sinner, but of Jesus on the cross.

In biblical justice, love is the foundation of justice. Concern for justice is not something added to love; it is the order which love requires.

Daniel Day Williams has written that we may summarize the biblical justice in this way:

> . . . the Bible sees the issues of human justice arising in the history of the Christian community as the people of God seek to bring peace and reconciliation to all men, and to show a special concern for the hurt, the needy, and the weak. Before God every Christian knows that he is the hurt, the needy, the weak person for whom there could be only condemnation, if there were no mercy in God's righteousness. Thus Paul asserts the foundation of all Christian consideration of the other, 'Have this mind among yourselves which you have in Christ Jesus, who . . . humbled himself and took the form of a servant and became obedient unto death, even death on a cross' (Philippians 2:5-8).

LOVE

Who, in the public mind, in this century, has lived a life that embodies the Christian faith? If you were to draw a list, surely at the top would appear the name of Toyohiko Kagawa, who died in 1960. He was a man associated with love, although his critics charged that he had no theology.

In the summer of 1971, I visited with Kagawa's widow in Tokyo. I asked her to share with me some of the memories of Kagawa. She told of his boyhood. He lost his father when he was four years old. His mother, who was a concubine, also soon died. The woman who took him was violent in her antagonism toward him. His childhood and youth were miserable.

But something came into Kagawa's life. He learned about Jesus Christ, and that led him to believe that God is love. Then, while still young, about fifteen, he had tuberculosis, and the doctors were certain he would die. He was told that, at most, he could not expect to live past twenty-four. He decided then that whatever days were left to him, he would dedicate to God and the slum people.

At the time he made a commitment to serve the poor, he was too weak for any physical activity except the coughing of blood. But he identified with and prayed with the poor. Then he came to feel that it was not enough to simply live with the poor and pray for them. They needed to be able to change their circumstances, to change the way they related to society. And he felt that if he really loved them, he would be a part of that change. Thus, he took the step into organizing consumer cooperatives, housing projects, and even helped in forming, after World War II, a political party.

"Love," said Kagawa, "is the explosion of the soul." When love exploded into action for this frail little Japanese man, Mrs. Kagawa said, many other Christians accused him of having no theology.

Those who live by love may not always appear as consistent as those who live by law. If we were to draw parallels on some of the things said about Jesus, I suppose they might read, "He has no theology. He knows the scriptures, but he disregards them, or he bends them." Jesus lived in a dialectic between love and law, and chose love as a priority.

Elton Trueblood wrote a book on *The Company of the Committed*, but as he concluded the book, after having emphasized commitment, he felt compelled to say that commitment is not enough, it is not sufficient. For the Christian, there is only one absolute and that absolute is love, genuine caring for the other person.

The central ritual for the Christian Church is the Eucharist. The brokenness of the Body is nowhere illustrated more than in our being unable to gather the whole Christian family around one table. Nevertheless, almost all Christians participate in communion, most responding to the invitation:

> All who are in love and fellowship with your neighbor, who do truly and earnestly repent of your sins, who humbly put your trust in Christ and desire his help that you may lead a holy life, draw near to God and receive these elements to your comfort, through Jesus Christ our Lord.

This is the traditional invitation in the church. But the order has been changed. Once the second part, dealing with repentance, came first. Now, before we think of repentance, or anything else, the very first thought goes to love of neighbor.

How do we assess whether we have love for our neighbor? Is it not in whether we do justice?

HUMILITY

Humility is the ability to appreciate what is of value, whether in the other person or in yourself.

In defining an idea, it is often helpful to eliminate—to say what a thing or a substance or an idea is *not*. Humility is not self-depreciation. Humility is not a song which has us asking with Isaac Watts:

> Would he devote that sacred head
> For such a worm as I?

To walk humbly does not mean to crawl with the worms. Christian humility walks tall, indeed, with a head stretched toward the heavens. To walk humbly does not mean the wearing of rags when the necessity is not there because of one's economic condition, or because of drama in prophetic witness, or because of the need to identify with the people. Christian humility can wear rags when necessary, but is more comfortable in modesty and convention, with expressions of personality done with some degree of subtlety. Humility affirms true value, not self-consciously directed toward the self or away from the self. As Frederick Buechner put it in *Wishful Thinking,* "True humility doesn't consist of thinking ill of yourself but of not thinking of yourself much differently from the way you'd be apt to think of anyone else."

Humility is a strange kind of possession. To claim it, to be aware that you have it, is to lose it. Strange paradox. So, in irony, some comment falls, "The thing in which we take greatest pride is our humility." Or another will jest, "Please notice how humble I am considering how great I am." Chrysostom, in the fourth century, advised, "Never be elated at thy humility." Then he clarified:

> Perhaps you laugh at the expression, as if humility could puff up. But be not surprised at it, it puffs up, when it is not genuine . . . When it is practiced to gain the favour of men, and not of God, that we may be praised, and be high-minded.

Given the history and character of the Brethren, I think it is probably true that we, more than most, are attracted to the virtue of humility, and thus, also, to the temptation to try to appear humble. There is a world of difference between trying to appear humble and actual humility.

The absence of humility is destructive to being a whole person. Spiritual pride, the assumption that I am more holy, more righteous than you, is probably the most destructive of all forces upon a fellowship of believers. Spiritual pride as the assumption that I know the nature of reality and others are ignorant or naive is widespread and destructive to mutual respect.

To walk humbly. What is the character of the humility with which we are to walk?

Humility is found in having a sense of indebtedness. It is to realize how much has come from other people. It is to be deliberately aware and appreciate what others have done for us.

Humility is found in having a sense of need. Humility assumes the need to learn and to understand. It has listening skills. When we cannot bear to sit and listen to another person, when we presume we can only teach and give, but cannot learn and receive, we are lacking in humility. To deliberately listen, to deliberately change roles if we are accustomed to leading, to deliberately be aware of the need to grow—these are to cultivate the possibility of humility.

Humility is found in a deep sense of self-worth. When we feel worthwhile without needing to acquire the best seats at the banquet (Luke 20:46) to make us appear worthwhile, then we are approaching humility. Humility does not look to position for validation.

Humility is found in the willingness to risk humiliation. That risk can be a deliberate act. It means a readiness to look foolish if the cause is right, if the concern is genuine. Jesus spoke of it in the Beatitude, "Blessed are you when men revile you and persecute you and utter all kinds of evil against you falsely on my account" (Matthew 5:11).

Humility is found in an attitude of reverence. A deep respect for the Holy is the origin of true humility. In becoming aware of that Spirit that is the force of life, and in bowing before that Spirit, there is a cultivation of humility.

Walking humbly has great promise. Jesus often speaks of the reversal of this world's order in the kingdom. Thus, humility is more satisfying in the long run. It is not a matter of great self-sacrifice. It is, rather, a matter of self-discovery.

CONCERNING THE MICAH TEXT

The passage opens with a question of how to come before God. What would be pleasing to God? The question relates first to sacrifices. It was assumed that anyone who would worship God would have a sacrifice. If one does not have a good sacrifice does it mean that one is separated from God? The question turns even to human sacrifice, reflecting the religious customs of the Near East wherein the first-born son would be sacrificed to the Deity, that Deity would send other children and prosperity.

No. A resounding no. God is not impressed with the quantity of things that are given in tribute. Rather, God has shown what is good: "to do justice, and to love kindness, and to walk humbly with your God."

Walter Brueggemann, Dean, Eden Theological Seminary, comments on this last verse, saying, "These three statements, first of all, are not arguments about how to be human, but they are polemical assertions about the nature of God." (From an unpublished exegesis of Micah 6:1-8) They describe the character of God and that to which God responds. Brueggemann finds in earlier Micah passages the alternatives. The alternative to doing justice is in Micah 2:2: "They covet fields and seize them; and houses, and take them away; they oppress a man and his house, a man and his inheritance." Coveting is the alternative to doing justice.

The alternative to loving kindness is in Micah 3:2: "Is it not for you to know justice?—you who hate the good and love the evil, who tear the skin from off my people, and their flesh from off their bones." To tear away at the neighbor is the alternative to loving kindness. The Annual Conference statement reads, "to love tenderly." I am assuming that is a translation from the Hebrew which the preparers of the statement preferred. Chris Bucher, an Old Testament student and a member of my congregation, tells me that the Hebrew word *chesed* which is translated by the Revised Standard Version as "kindness" and by Annual Conference as "tenderly," has a wide range of meaning in the Old Testament and consequently, no simple English equivalent. The Old Testament uses the word *chesed* to describe the action of God, as well as human action. When *chesed* refers to human activity, as in this text, it generally designates the act of a person in power or in a superior position, politically or economically, in behalf of an individual lacking power or status. An act of *chesed* can be an offer of protection or an act of deliverance. It usually occurs between parties who are related in community or covenant and indicates the acceptance of responsibility for each other. *Chesed* as the steadfast love of one human being for another ultimately manifests one's responsibility before God.

The alternative to walking humbly is in Micah 2:3-8, which says that the people of God "shall not walk haughtily." If we assume with Brueggemann that this Micah description is, first of all, concerned with the nature of God, then "to walk humbly" takes away the "macho" image of God, and makes God more like what we know of Jesus Christ. That is, God's power is in weakness; God's glory is in the cross.

There are places in scripture where the message is fundamental, where there is a simple and clear definition of what it means to be a Christian. One of those is in John 13:35, where Jesus declares that you will be known as his disciple "if you have love for one another." Another is in Matthew 25, in the parable of the Last Judgment where Jesus says that those who are saved are those who give food to the hungry and drink to the thirsty, who welcome the stranger, who give clothing to the naked, and who visit the sick and those in prison. Certainly, here in Micah is to be found also a very basic, fundamental religious faith. What the Lord requires is for you to do justice, to love tenderly, to walk humbly with your God.

CONCERNING THE HYMN

What better way to conclude a study of the mission factor of the church than to sing a hymn? How better face the decade than with a song from your throat?

Harry Emerson Fosdick's hymn, "God of Grace and God of Glory" is a favorite of mine and when sung in our congregations and at Annual Conference, it both expresses our faith and beckons to our faith. The hymn, I believe, is an appropriate prayer for the 1980's. Consider the various lines. Note especially the third verse that voices confession and concern for war, pride, selfishness, and the opposite of the simple life.

For the decade of the 1980's, we will do well to sing and pray,

> Grant us wisdom,
> Grant us courage,
> For the facing of this hour.

FOR FURTHER CONSIDERATION

• If you concur that justice has not been a dominant theme with the Brethren, why do you think it is the case?

• Do you find it easier to witness for peace or to serve the poor than to actively engage in justice issues?

• Who are the peoples who today suffer the greatest injustices in our society? Illegal immigrants? Women? Criminals? The poor? Homosexuals? Racial minorities? Taxpayers?

• Identify things that need to be made right.

• Is your congregational life marked by justice?

• How is loving tenderly related to the five goals listed under that heading?

• What characterizes the people you see as possessing humility?

SOME ACTIVITIES

Study the agencies of justice in your community to determine whether justice is being served in your courts and your prisons. Review with your related church commission or Church Board your ministry to prisoners.

Plan a role reversal session in which those who usually lead are listeners, and those who usually just listen, give leadership.

Plan a forum on justice issues related to the media, exploring such issues as censorship, violence, sex exploitation, access, commercialization, character assassination.

RESOURCES FOR ADDITIONAL STUDY

Coffin, William Sloan, Jr. *Once to Every Man.* Paterson, N.J.: Atheneum, 1977.

Ellul, Jacques. *The Politics of God and the Politics of Man.* Grand Rapids: Eerdmans, 1972.

Engage/Social Action, December, 1979.

Heschel, Abraham J. *The Prophets.* New York: Harper-Row, 1962.

King, Martin Luther, Jr. *Stride Toward Freedom.* New York: Harper-Row, 1958.

Williams, Daniel Day. *The Spirit and the Forms of Love,* especially Chapter 12. New York: Harper-Row, 1968.

WATCH

A NOVEL

KEITH BUCKLEY

WATCH

A NOVEL

a barnacle book | rare bird books
los angeles, calif.

A Genuine Barnacle Book

A Barnacle Book | Rare Bird Books
453 South Spring Street, Suite 302
Los Angeles, CA 90013
rarebirdbooks.com

FIRST TRADE PAPERBACK ORIGINAL EDITION

Set in Dante
Printed in the United States

10 9 8 7 6 5 4 3 2 1

Publisher's Cataloging-in-Publication data
Names: Buckley, Keith, author.
Title: Watch : a novel / Keith Buckley.
Description: First Trade Paperback Original Edition |
A Genuine Barnacle Book | New York, NY; Los Angeles, CA:
Rare Bird Books, 2018.
Identifiers: ISBN 9781947856479
Subjects: LCSH Relationships—Fiction. | Family—Fiction. | Time—
Fiction. | Death—Fiction. | BISAC FICTION / Literary
Classification: LCC PS3602.U2624 W38 2018 | DDC 813.6—dc23